NA FIANNA ÉIREANN IN CORK CITY AND THE FIGHT FOR IRISH INDEPENDENCE (1910-1921)

Colmán de Róiste, M.A.

ORLA KELLY PUBLISHING

978-1-915502-60-5

Cover design by 2funkidesign.com. Published in Ireland by Orla Kelly Publishing.

Orla Kelly Publishing
27 Kilbrody,
Mount Oval,
Rochestown,
Cork,
Ireland.

To Hanna

About the Author

Cork author Colmán de Róiste holds an MA in Military History from the University of Wolverhampton. He wrote his Masters dissertation on Na Fianna Éireann in Cork city (1910-1921).

Colmán is the Grandson of Denis Woods, a former Officer Commanding (O/C) a Fianna Company in Cork City during the War of Independence, and he is the Great Nephew of Christopher Woods, also a former O/C of a Fianna Company in Cork City and subsequently the Intelligence Officer (1921) for the Cork city-based B Company of the 1st Battalion, Cork No. 1 Brigade.

List of Abbreviations

AOH	Ancient Order of Hibernians
ASU	Active Service Unit
CO	Commanding Officer
Col.	Colonel
Comdt.	Commandant (Irish equivalent of a British Army Major)
Div.	Division
Gen.	General
GHQ	General Headquarters
IRA	Irish Republican Army
IRB	Irish Republican Brotherhood
IV	Irish Volunteers
Lt.	Lieutenant (Irish)
O/C	Officer Commanding
RIC	Royal Irish Constabulary
TD	Teachta Dála (Deputy of the Dáil)
Vol.	Volunteer

Glossary of Irish terms used in the text

Ard Choiste	Executive (lit. High Committee)
Ard Chomhairle	Central Council (lit. High Council)
Ard Fheinne	High Commander of the Fianna
Ard Fheis (pl. Ard Fheiseanna)	Convention (lit. High Gathering)
Ard Thaoiseach	Chief Scout (lit. High Chief)
Buachaill (pl. Buachaillí)	Boy
Céilí	Evening entertainment (dancing and music)
An Céad Slua	The First Troop (lit. The First Host)
Clann na hÉireann	Children of Ireland
Clann na Gael	Children of the Gael
Clann na Poblachta	Children of the Republic
Comrac	Struggle
Cumann na mBan	The Women's Association
Dáil	Parliament (lit. assembly)
Dáil Éireann	The Irish Parliament
Éire	Ireland
Feis (pl. Feiseanna)	Convention / Gathering

Fian (pl. Fiannaí)	Member of the Fianna
Fianna Éireann	Army of Ireland
Fianna Fáil	Army of Destiny
Fianna na hÉireann Óg	Army of Young Ireland
Fine Gael	Tribe of the Gael
Garda	Policeman (Ireland)
Na Fianna	The Fianna (Army)
Nodlaig na bhFiann	The Fian's Christmas
Óglach	Soldier
Óglaigh na hÉireann	Soldiers of Ireland
Oireachtas	Assembly
An Phoblacht	The Republic
Poblacht na hÉireann	The Republic of Ireland
Sinn Féin	Ourselves
Slua (pl. Sluaite)	Troop (lit. host)

Acknowledgments

I would like to thank several people without whose contributions I could not have completed this book. Firstly, I would like to thank my uncle Donnacha and my sister Majella who provided me with my grandfather Denis Woods' handwritten notes, letters, and typed correspondence from his time as Na Fianna Éireann secretary for Cork city during the 1930s and the early 1940s. These notes formed the building blocks of this book and originally inspired me to research and seek out more information on the history of the Cork city Fianna.

I would like to thank Dr Eamonn O'Kane, who I was fortunate to have as my dissertation supervisor at the University of Wolverhampton for my M.A. thesis in Military History, for which 'Na Fianna Éireann in Cork city 1910 – 1921' was my chosen subject.

Special thanks must be given to my sister Sharon, my brother in-law John, my niece Katie and my nephew Dylan who visited the Military Archives in Dublin to assist me in the research on the republican activities of Denis Woods and his Cork city Fianna comrades during the Irish War of Independence.

I'd like to thank my friend Stephen Glennon for his help in editing the final version of this book and providing much-welcomed constructive feedback.

I would like to thank all the people who scoured their memories and provided me with their recollections, photos, and documents to help add to the material in this book. These people include Sheila Boyle and her daughter Patricia (daughter and granddaughter of the former Cork city Fianna Adjutant Dan Scully), my uncle Noel, my mother's first cousin Anna, and John Watts, who wrote his 1981 PhD thesis at the University of Glasgow on 'Na Fianna Éireann: A Case Study of a Political Youth Organisation'.

Author's Note

My aim in the writing of this book was to research and examine the contribution of the Cork city branch of Na Fianna Éireann towards the revolutionary movement for Irish independence from British rule during the period of the formation of Na Fianna Éireann in Cork in 1910 up until the declaration of the ceasefire of hostilities – 'The Truce' – on July 11, 1921.

The motivation behind choosing this topic was my observation that Na Fianna Éireann as an organisation has been consistently overlooked as a topic of study in academic works that focus on the independence movement in Cork. Whilst recent studies exist on the subject of Na Fianna Éireann as a national organisation, I have observed a gap in the literature concerning the activities and operations of Na Fianna Éireann in Cork city.

I was enabled to launch a detailed research study into this topic due to my personal access to information documents and correspondence of my maternal grandfather Denis Woods, who served both as an Officer Commanding (O/C) of B Company, First Battalion, Na Fianna Éireann, Cork city during the period 1920 to 1921 and as the Honourable Secretary, Na Fianna Éireann, Cork, during the period 1934 to 1943. In addition, I was able to fully utilise the public access to both the paper and online collections of the Irish Military Archives in Dublin, which contain a considerable collection of Cork IRA and Cork Fianna Éireann veteran witness statements, operations documents and pension and medal applications for military service spanning the Irish revolutionary period of 1916 to 1921.

Colmán de Róiste,

January 02, 2024

Contents

Introduction

On 09 July 1942, Denis Woods, the Honourable Secretary for Na Fianna Éireann, Cork, wrote to M. Cummins, Office of the Defence, Military Service Pension Board appealing for recognition for the Fianna members in Cork city who supported the Cork IRA during the Irish War of Independence (normally considered as 21 January 1919 (The Soloheadbeg Ambush) to 11 July 1921 (Date of Truce)). Mr Woods stated, "we cannot understand the reason why your board has not recognised the Fianna in Cork as one of the military organisations that were responsible for that measure of freedom this country gained as a result of the combined actions of these organisations (IRA). Up to date only two officers of the Fianna in Cork have been given an award" (Appendix 2).

To clarify, the aim of this book is not to attempt a detailed examination of the intricacies of the administration and bureaucracy of the successive Irish Military Service Pension boards of the 1920s to 1950s, which has been described by the historian Marie Coleman as "a system of political patronage that many subsequently saw as reflecting discreditably upon the revolutionary generation".[1] Instead, the aim of this book is to address an examination of what Mr Woods had termed "the combined actions" of Na Fianna Éireann and the Irish Republican Army (IRA) within the specific context of the area of Cork city during this period and in the formative revolutionary years preceding it. For the period of the Irish War of Independence, Cork city was included as part of the area under the military responsibility of the IRA First Cork Brigade. The city area was represented by two battalions, an active service unit and a special intelligence section. Although a separate organisation, during the years 1911 to 1921 Na Fianna Éireann in

---

1 Coleman, Marie, 'Military Service Pension for Veterans of the Irish Revolution, 1916-1923', War in History, April 2013, Vol. 20, No. 2 (April 2013), p. 220, Sage Publications Ltd.

Cork city became increasingly linked and collaborative in terms of its support, propaganda and ultimately its military operations with firstly the city branch of the Irish Volunteers and who subsequently developed into the Irish Republican Army. This interlinkage of these two organisations culminated in a situation that by 1920 saw a transfer rate of senior Cork Fianna boys to the IRA First Cork Brigade allegedly far exceeding that of fifty percent,[2] as well as the formation of an Active Service Unit of the Cork city Fianna whose primary function was "to have lads available for any sudden call from the IRA".[3]

To date, no specific study has been written on the composition, function, and activities of the Cork Fianna, either in the city or Cork County as a whole. The historian John Borgonova writes how Cork was "the most violent county in Ireland…over-represented in various measurements of revolutionary intensity".[4] Similarly, the historian Peter Hart wrote of Cork as "the most violent of all Irish counties in the troubles".[5] Hart described his 1998 work 'The IRA & Its Enemies – Violence and Community in Cork 1916-1923' as "a study of the rise and fall of the revolutionary movement within a single county",[6] but only briefly refers to Na Fianna Éireann in Cork in just two lines within this book of 315 pages. Additional modern studies of Cork during this period such as William Sheehan's 2011 book 'A Hard Local War – The British Army and The Guerrilla War in Cork 1919-1921' do not include any mention of Na Fianna Éireann. In 'Rebel Cork's Fighting Story 1916-1921 – Told by The Men Who Made It', the four-page final chapter is titled and devoted to another IRA support organisation, 'Cumann na mBan in Rebel Cork', yet in the entire published content Na Fianna Éireann is only briefly mentioned in just three sentences.

---

2 Watts, John R. (1981) 'Na Fianna Éireann: A Case Study of a Political Youth Organisation', University of Glasgow, p. 166.

3 George Hurley, B.M.H. witness statement, July 15, 1957. (N.A.I., B.M.H, WS 1630), p. 5.

4 Crowley, John, O'Drisceoil, Donal & Murphy, Mike (2017) 'Atlas of The Irish Revolution', New York University Press, p. 558

5 Hart, Peter (1999), 'The I.R.A. & Its Enemies – Violence and Community in Cork 1916-1923', Clarendon Press, Oxford, p. vii.

6 Ibid, p. vii.

Marie Coleman in her 2013 article 'Military Service Pensions for Veterans of the Irish Revolution, 1916-1923', wrote of the online release by the Irish Military Archives of military pension and medal applications over the Irish Revolutionary period that "the greatest benefit of the pensions will possibly be to historians: the release of such a considerable archive of personal narratives, contemporary documents, and brigade compilations of events and personnel lists of the revolutionary period…throw considerably more light on the men and women who fought for Irish independence".[7] This book intends to extend that light to provide focus on the boys of Cork city who also fought for Irish independence and to offer an examination of both the formation and contribution of the members of this youth organisation who Denis Woods described as "few if any of them having reached their twenties on the 11th July 1921" (Appendix 2).

The primary research undertaken for this book involved a detailed examination of the pension and medal application files of multiple former members of the Cork city Fianna. These files were obtained both online and at the Office of the Irish Military Archives in Dublin. This research was combined with the study of multiple witness statements of former Cork city Fianna and IRA members taken by the Irish Bureau of Military History in the late 1940s to 1950s, concerning the revolutionary period in Ireland from 1913 to 1921. In addition, this author has had the privilege of access to the private notes, papers and correspondence of Denis Woods, Honourable Secretary for Na Fianna Éireann, Cork during the period 1933 to 1943.

Another important source of information was the 1981 PhD thesis of John Watts, University of Glasgow, 'Na Fianna Éireann: A Case Study of a Political Youth Organisation'. As part of the primary research for his thesis Mr Watts conducted separate private interviews with three former Cork city Fianna in the summer of 1979 – John Murray, George Hurley, and Seán Healy. Mr Watts spoke with this author on Thursday, 30 November 2017 and shared his personal notes and recollections of these three interviews.

---

7 Coleman, Marie, 'Military Service Pension for Veterans of the Irish Revolution, 1916-1923', War in History, April 2013, Vol. 20, No. 2 (April 2013), p. 221, Sage Publications Ltd.

The witness statements obtained by the Bureau of Military History in the 1940s and 1950s primarily contain witness accounts on the revolutionary period in Ireland from 1913 to 1921. Due to this fact, combined with witness reports that the Cork city Fianna and the City's Irregular forces (Anti-Treaty IRA) essentially acted as one military body in terms of operations during the Irish Civil War, this book is then solely concerned with the contribution of Na Fianna Éireann in Cork city against British Rule (i.e., to the date of the Truce – 11 July 1921).

George Hurley (left, circa 1920), serving with G Company, First Battalion
George Hurley (right, circa 1960) Honourable Secretary, Na Fianna Éireann, Cork

Denis Woods (photo circa 1950)
Former Officer Commanding (O/C) B Company, First Battalion, Na Fianna Éireann, Cork city, 1920 –
1921, and Honourable Secretary, Na Fianna Éireann, Cork, 1934 – 1943.

Cork city Fianna attendees at The Munster Fianna Convention held in the grounds of Technical School, Cork city on 16 April 1922.

Top Row Left to Right (Names confirmed by The Cork Public Museum):

1. *Denis Woods, Officer Commanding, B Company, First Battalion*
2. *Edward Murray, Officer Commanding, Second Battalion*
3. *Dan Mulroy, Officer Commanding, First Battalion*
4. *Patrick Lynch, Officer Commanding, D Company, First Battalion*
5. *Stephen Walsh, Officer Commanding, A Company, First Battalion*
6. *Patrick Carey, Rank unknown,*
7. *Person name unknown,*
8. *William Quirke, Officer Commanding, C Company, Second Battalion*
9. *James Wickham, Adjutant, B Company, First Battalion*

Left - Vincent Stack, First Lieutenant, E Company, First Battalion
Right - (standing behind person unknown) Jeremiah Pierce, First Lieutenant, G Company, First Battalion

Robert Flynn (left), First Lieutenant, B Company, First Battalion
Daniel Gamble (middle), Officer Commanding, G Company, First Battalion
Charles Meaney (right), Officer Commanding, H Company, Second Battalion

Stephen Wall (circa 1920), Officer Commanding, D Company, First Battalion

MUNSTER FIANNA ÉIREANN TREATY DEBATE 1922 (Full Image)

The meeting was held in Cork by representatives of Na Fianna Éireann in the Munster area.

They had gathered to debate the 1921 Anglo-Irish Treaty. Their final vote was to reject the Treaty and subsequently many Fianna fought on the anti-Treaty side in the Civil War.

Two delegates from Fianna GHQ in Dublin attended: Barney Mellows and Frank McMahon (both pictured front centre with Fianna flag resting on their knees).

CHAPTER ONE

The origins of Na Fianna Éireann

Na Fianna Éireann (or the Irish Nationalist Boy Scouts) was an Irish nationalist youth organisation founded by Bulmer Hobson (1883-1969) and Countess Constance Markievicz (1868-1927) on 16 August 1909 at 34 Lower Camden Street, Dublin.[8] Hobson and Markievicz established the organisation with the aim to provide a nationalist antidote to the growing popularity of British uniformed groups in Ireland, such as Sir Robert Baden-Powell's Boy Scout movement. In an article published in 1914 in Na Fianna Éireann's Christmas magazine 'Nodlaig na bhFianna', Markievicz recounted how she had read a review in the Irish Times of Baden-Powell Boy Scout's by the Lord Lieutenant at Clontarf, recalling that "the idea of those young Irish lads haunted me".[9] The countess recognised the effectiveness of Baden-Powell's Scouts in fostering loyalty in youth to the British flag and "believing that its methods might be used with comparable success in the cause of separatism, made up her mind to found a nationalist boy scout movement".[10] Hobson had formed an earlier "Fianna" in 1902 to serve as a Junior Hurling League and to promote the study of the Irish Language at the Catholic Boys' Hall, Falls Road, in West Belfast. After Hobson later relocated to Dublin, the Fianna organisation had collapsed in Belfast. The historian Marnie Hay writes "Upon hearing about Hobson's Belfast Fianna, Markievicz declared

---

8 Crowley, John, O'Drisceoil, Donal & Murphy, Mike (2017) 'Atlas of The Irish Revolution', New York University Press, p. 173.

9 Watts, John R. (1981) 'Na Fianna Éireann: A Case Study of a Political Youth Organisation', University of Glasgow, p. 19.

10 Ibid, p. 19.

that a national boys organisation should be established in Dublin in the same spirit as the original group".[11]

The new organisation was created as the militarised reincarnation of the original 1902 'Fianna'. Hobson, a Belfast Quaker, was in 1909 just 26 years old and was already a prominent Sinn Féin propagandist and rising member of the Irish Republican Brotherhood (IRB). Marnie Hay states how Markievicz, in order to make her vision a reality, required Hobson's organisational experience, the template of his previous boys' group, and his IRB connections. Hobson, on the other hand, to create his vision of a strong youth force to help in the liberation of Ireland, required Markievicz's initial injection of money, as well as her energy, enthusiasm and, due to her gender and social position, her ability to gain the trust of the parents of the younger boys.[12]

Hobson chaired the meeting on 16 August 1909, in the Camden Street Hall, to "form a National Boys Organisation to be managed by the boys themselves on national non-party lines".[13]

In his opening meeting address, Hobson outlined that the organisation would be run on a semi-military basis along similar lines to the Baden Powell Boy Scouts movement. Indeed, it was an immediate objective of Na Fianna Éireann to counteract the national influence in Ireland of Baden-Powell's pro-British body. Among those present at this inaugural meeting of the Fianna was a fifteen-year-old boy called Michael Lonergan. In a military witness statement taken in 1948, he described this meeting as "the beginning – militarily – of the events leading up to Easter Week".[14] Marnie Hay writes how the Fianna in Dublin were "the first nationalist group in Ireland to begin drilling; it went on to train members of the IRB, and its members were among the few men, other

11 Hay, Marnie, 'The foundation and development of Na Fianna Éireann, 1909-16', Irish Historical Studies, xxxvi, no. 141 (May 2008), p. 55.

12 Ibid, pp. 55-56.

13 Ibid, p. 56.

14 Michael Lonergan, B.M.H. witness statement, 1 Aug, 1948 (N.A.I., B.M.H., WS 140).

than ex-British soldiers, to possess the military training necessary to become officers when the Irish Volunteers was formed in 1913".[15]

Following the inaugural meeting in August 1909, 'An Céad Slua' – the first Fianna troop – was formed. The troop members met regularly in those initial years in the Camden Street Hall where they adopted a jersey and kilt as their uniform. Marnie Hay outlines how the troop's activities included the training of the boys in elementary drill, route marching, learned signalling, first aid, and other scouting skills such as map reading, path-finding and elementary astronomy. The boys were also taught the Irish language and Irish history, with an emphasis on the history of Irish battles and insurrections, with the purpose of instilling in the boys the rationale for their own military training. [16]

The formal organisational structure of Na Fianna Éireann from its formation consisted of an Executive (including a president, two vice presidents, an honorary secretary, an honorary assistant secretary, and an honorary treasurer), an ard-fheis (congress), an ard-choisde (central council), district councils and sluaighte (troops). The ard-fheis met annually and served as the supreme governing and legislative body of Na Fianna Éireann. The ard-choisde provided the general direction of Na Fianna Éireann and it also served as the governing body of the organisation when the ard-fheis was not sitting.[17]

Another attendee of the inaugural meeting in August 1909 was Eamon Martin, who in later life described in his military witness statement the national growth of the organisation following its initial formative years: "by 1913, the organisation had spread beyond the Dublin region to Belfast, Cork, Limerick, Derry, Waterford, Clonmel, Dundalk, Newry, Listowel and Glasgow".[18]

---

15 Hay, Marnie, 'The foundation and development of Na Fianna Éireann, 1909-16', Irish Historical Studies, xxxvi, no. 141 (May 2008), p. 56.

16 Ibid, p.58.

17 The Central Council of Na Fianna Éireann (1914), 'Fianna Handbook', p. 15.

18 Eamon Martin, B.M.H. witness statement, n.d. (N.A.I., B.M.H, WS 591).

CHAPTER TWO

The Growth of Na Fianna Éireann
in Cork city (1910-1914)

P.J. Murphy, a former Company Commander of Na Fianna Éireann, in his 1953 Bureau of Military History witness statement declared Cork city at the beginning of the twentieth century as "known throughout the length and breadth of the land as "Rotten Cork" and "Khaki Cork" – names which made every honest Nationalist in the city blush with shame. There was little or no political activity at the time but displays of loyalty to England were everywhere".[19] The Gaelic cultural revival of the late nineteenth and early twentieth century had led to the formation of organisations such as the 'Cork Celtic Literary Society' (the first nationalist organisation founded in Cork), the Gaelic Athletic Association (GAA) and Conradh na Gaeilge (Gaelic League). Cork members of the Irish Republican Brotherhood (IRB) began to infiltrate these organisations in great numbers in the opening years of the new century and hence local republicans began to build up a network.[20]

According to the Bureau of Military History witness statement of James Allan Busby taken on 06 June 1957, Busby, who had once held the rank of First Lieutenant with Na Fianna Éireann in Cork city, stated that it was in 1911 when he attended the first meeting for to establish a branch of Na Fianna Éireann in Cork.[21] This was held in the Dun on Queen Street. Graham Harrington, in his article

---

19 .J. Murphy, B.M.H. witness statement, April 14, 1953. (N.A.1., B.M.H., WS 869), p. 1.
20 'THE HISTORY OF NA FIANNA ÉIREANN IN CORK CITY 1910-1924' https://FiannaÉireannhistory. wordpress.com/2016/10/06/the-history-of-na-Fianna-Éireann-in-cork-city-1910-1924/, accessed June 22, 2022.
21 James Allan Busby, B.M.H. witness statement, June 06, 1957. (N.A.I., B.M.H., WS 1628), p. 1.

'Na Fianna Éireann in Cork city, 1910-1924', cites the year of the organisation's formation in Cork as 1910.[22] Both accounts concur that Na Fianna Éireann in Cork was established by republicans involved in the O'Growney Branch of the Gaelic League: "Its key organisers included: Tomás Mac Curtain, Seán O'Hegarty, Seán O'Sullivan, Paddy Corkery, Miceal Ó Cuill, Tadhg Barry, Martin Donovan, Miceall O'Neill, Donnchadh O'Donnaghue, and Ned Rochford. Walter Furlong was appointed the first scoutmaster in the city. Seán O'Sullivan was elected secretary and Tomás Mac Curtain was elected treasurer. These were the main organisers in the city up until members joined the Irish Volunteers which was established in 1913".[23] Busby recounted how, subsequent to the initial meetings held on Queen Street, a sluagh of Na Fianna Éireann was formed in Cork city with Christy Moynihan as its scout master (captain). "In the early days, i.e., prior to 1916, we had one sluagh only in the city...... we drilled in the Dun, held route marches and went to the country in the summer for field work at Blarney and elsewhere outside the city".[24] The initial recruitment for Na Fianna Éireann in Cork city prior to 1912 has been described as "gradual".[25] P.J. Murphy stated that the Fianna in Cork in 1912 was not a very popular organisation – plenty of opposition existed from the Baden Powell scout movement and the AOH Boys' Brigade, whose headquarters were in the South Mall and Morrison's Island, which was within just two hundred yards of the Fianna headquarters at the time on Queen Street.[26] The AOH Boys Brigade stood for the boys' brigade of the 'Ancient Order of Hibernians', an organisation first formed in Ulster from the Catholic agrarian movements of the eighteen and nineteenth centuries. By 1912, membership of the AOH had spread throughout Ireland and the organisation

22 'THE HISTORY OF NA FIANNA ÉIREANN IN CORK CITY 1910-1924' https://FiannaÉireannhistory. wordpress.com/2016/10/06/the-history-of-na-Fianna-Éireann-in-cork-city-1910-1924/, accessed June 22, 2022.
23 Ibid, accessed June 22, 2022.
24 James Allan Busby, B.M.H. witness statement, June 06, 1957. (N.A.I., B.M.H, WS 1628), p. 2.
25 'THE HISTORY OF NA FIANNAA ÉIREANN IN CORK CITY 1910-1924' https://FiannaÉireannhistory. wordpress.com/2016/10/06/the-history-of-na-Fianna-Éireann-in-cork-city-1910-1924/, accessed June 22, 2022.
26 P.J. Murphy, B.M.H. witness statement, April 14, 1953. (N.A.1., B.M.H., WS 869), p. 4.

was closely linked with the Irish Parliamentary Party.[27] Robert Baden Powell, a British army officer had established the Boy Scouts movement in Britain in 1908. The Boy Scouts movement placed an emphasis on outdoor activities and the personal development in male adolescents of traits such as discipline, trust, obedience, loyalty, service, and self-sacrifice. Marie Hay writes how Na Fianna Éireann sought to promote these same qualities but "in an Irish nationalist rather than British imperialist context. The Irish organisation offered its members a combination of military training, outdoor activities and cultural endeavours".[28]

In 1912, a group of twelve Cork city boys, including Liam O'Callaghan and Christy Moynihan, decided to leave the Baden Powell Scouts and join the Fianna. Their decision was made following a trip to Dublin with the Scouts for the King's visit to that city. While in Dublin, O'Callaghan and Moynihan contacted the Fianna and received instruction on how to join the organisation's branch in Cork. By the end of 1912 there were about thirty boys in Na Fianna Éireann in Cork city, and the strength continued to grow after that.[29] Moynihan has been described as "an excellent scoutmaster and very efficient in all scouting subjects. Training was given in map reading, knots, morse, semaphore, first aid, tent pitching, tracking and scoutcraft generally. Tests were held at intervals and the Scoutmaster was very strict in maintaining a high standard in them".[30]

From its inception, Bulmer Hobson and Countess Markievicz had purported Na Fianna Éireann to be a national, non-party organisation open to all Irish boys from the ages of eight to eighteen regardless of class, creed, or party that they or their fathers belonged to. Hobson's long-term aim was to recruit suitable members of the new Fianna into the IRB. Hence, the organisation had over time become more openly militant and began to serve as a training ground for future adult members of the IRB and later Irish Volunteers. In July 1912, at the third annual

---

27 'Make way for the Molly Maguires!' The Ancient Order of Hibernians and the Irish Parliamentary Party, 1902–14' https://www.historyireland.com/make-way-for-the-molly-maguires-the-ancient-order-of-hibernians-and-the-irish-parliamentary-party-1902-14/, accessed June 22, 2022.

28 Hay, Marnie, 'The foundation and development of Na Fianna Éireann, 1909-16', Irish Historical Studies, xxxvi, no. 141 (May 2008), p. 54.

29 Seán Healy & Liam O'Callaghan, B.M.H. witness statement, October 04, 1947. (N.A.I., B.M.H, WS 47), p. 2.

30 Ibid, p. 2.

ard-fheis of Na Fianna Éireann, the organisation's constitution was amended to "assert that the object of the Fianna was to re-establish the independence of Ireland, and that this object was to be achieved through 'the training of the youth of Ireland, mentally and physically…by teaching scouting and military exercises, Irish history, and the Irish language'. Members promised 'to work for the Independence of Ireland, never to join England's armed forces, and to obey [their] superior officers".[31] An example of the openly militant rhetoric that the adult leaders of the Fianna impressed on their young members can be seen from an incident described by P.J. Murphy from the summer of 1913 when the Cork City Fianna had a visit from Countess Markievicz, Liam Mellows and Eamonn Martin. Murphy wrote how the Countess carried an automatic revolver "she produced the revolver and told us how anxious she was to use it in the fight for freedom".[32] Murphy continued in his account to say that it was around this time that the Fianna began to drill with wooden rifles instead of the scout poles they had used previously.

In addition to their scouting and training exercises, these early years of 1912 and 1913 saw the Cork city Fianna act as a guard of honour for the Blessed Sacrament at Wilton Church during the annual public procession and the Fianna also performed the laying of laurel wreaths on Fenian graves on the day of the annual Manchester Martyrs commemoration in Cork.[33]

---

31 Hay, Marnie, 'The foundation and development of Na Fianna Éireann, 1909-16', Irish Historical Studies, xxxvi, no. 141 (May 2008), pp. 59-60.

32 P.J. Murphy, B.M.H. witness statement, April 14, 1953. (N.A.1., B.M.H., WS 869), p. 4.

33 'THE HISTORY OF NA FIANNAA ÉIREANN IN CORK CITY 1910-1924' https://FiannaaÉireannhistory. wordpress.com/2016/10/06/the-history-of-na-Fianna-Éireann-in-cork-city-1910-1924/, accessed June 22, 2022.

CHAPTER THREE

Na Fianna Éireann in Cork city and The Irish Volunteers (1913 -1915)

Eoin MacNeil, one of the founders of the Irish Volunteers, was once asked how the revolution in Ireland had been brought about, "Mainly by Carson",[34] he replied. What MacNeil had meant by this was that in 1912 Edward Carson and the Ulster Unionists began their campaign against Home Rule, which led in January 1913 to the creation of the Ulster Volunteer Force (UVF). The creation of the UVF (the process of organising an army) served as an incentive and an example for militant activities in the rest of Ireland: the UVF provided a model for the creation of a more powerful army: the 'Irish Volunteers'.[35] By July 1913, Bulmer Hobson was serving as the chairperson of the Dublin Board of the IRB Centres and as the editor of the IRB newspaper 'Irish Freedom'. At a meeting of the Dublin board that month, Hobson proposed the establishment of a national military volunteer organisation. The first meeting of the 'Irish National Volunteers' was held on 25 November 1913, at the Rotunda Rink in Dublin.[36] Eoin MacNeil presided over the meeting and made the opening speech. Reports estimated that of the 7,000 attendees present, some 3,000 men enrolled in the Irish Volunteers. A manifesto, outlining the aims and policy of the Irish Volunteers, was issued on the first night – with the principal aim "to safeguard the rights of Irish people".[37] The Volunteers adopted "Defence, not Defiance" as their motto. A provisional

---

34 Tierney, Mark (1987), 'Ireland since 1870', C J Fallon, p. 155.

35 Ibid, p. 155.

36 Ibid, pp. 156-157.

37 Ibid, p. 157

committee of thirty was set up to organise the running of the Volunteers. Of this thirty, twelve members were provided by the IRB. Bulmer Hobson was one of these twelve men.

In Cork city, the Irish Volunteers were first formed on 14 December 1913, with their headquarters established in the Corn Market. Their initial meeting was held in the City Hall. The chairman of the Cork County GAA board, Mr. J.J. Walsh presided over the meeting and at his invitation the meeting was addressed by the guest speakers Eoin MacNeil (leader of the Irish Volunteers) and Sir Roger Casement.[38] According to reports, City Hall was at full capacity with standing room only as crowds clamoured to hear the speakers. Na Fianna Éireann had a small and uniformed presence on the stage. MacNeil's speech provoked a hostile reaction from some members of the crowd – he had praised the Ulster Volunteers for setting 'the model and standard of public duty'[39] for Irish people to follow. When MacNeill finished his speech a number of those booing then pushed forward to the front of the stage aggressively: "J.J Walsh was knocked to the floor when a chair was whipped across the head. The chairman's table was raised up and flung across the hall where it landed in the middle of the floor and broke in two. The boys of Fianna Éireann who had been on the stage for ceremonial purposes were now serving as bodyguards to the guest speakers and formed a protective circle around both Casement and MacNeill".[40] Seán Healy recalled of the incident that the Fianna boys present "did their best to prevent the hostile crowd getting on to the platform when the row started. In fact, Christy Moynihan saved the Chairman J.J. Walsh from more serious injury by breaking a blow intended for him".[41] The Cork historian Donal O'Drisceoil states this reaction was almost inevitable due to the fact that the members of the 'Ancient Order of Hibernians' (AOH) – who he describes as the shock troops of the Irish Parliamentary party – had positioned themselves at the front of the

---

38 'Rowdy rebels - the formation of the Irish Volunteers in Cork city', https://www.irishcentral.com/roots/history/rowdy-rebels-formation-irish-volunteers-cork-city, accessed June 22, 2022.

39 Ibid, accessed June 22, 2022.

40 Ibid, accessed June 22, 2022.

41 Seán Healy & Liam O'Callaghan, B.M.H. witness statement, October 04, 1947. (N.A.I., B.M.H, WS 47), p. 3.

stage. At this time, John Redmond (leader of the Irish Parliamentary Party) had not endorsed the Irish Volunteers and in fact the Volunteers were seen as a threat to the authority of the Irish Parliamentary Party.[42] According to Cork Historian Gerry White "when Eoin MacNeil finished his speech calling for three cheers for the Ulster Volunteers all hell broke loose".[43] Despite the violent scenes that had disrupted the proceedings, the meeting did result in over 400 men present signing up to join the Irish Volunteers.

From the inaugural meeting onwards close contact between the Fianna and the Irish Volunteers in Cork city was maintained. Na Fianna member Seán Healy led the Volunteers first public parade, where he played the bagpipes. On St Patrick's Day 1914, the Irish Volunteers, Na Fianna Éireann, Cumann na mBan and Clan na Gael combined to march in "one of the biggest parades held in the city".[44] Detachments of Cork Fianna were sent with the Volunteers to training camps at locations such as Mitchelstown, where they assisted with putting up tents and cooking. Fianna members also protested with Volunteers against Cork theatres showing British recruiting films, usually by battering the cinema screen with eggs. Na Fianna member Liam O'Callaghan immediately transferred to the Volunteers upon their formation and became a section leader. In alignment with Bulmer Hobson's original aim for Na Fianna Éireann members to eventually transition into the IRB, the older boys of the Fianna in Cork city were regularly transferring to the Irish Volunteers.

The outbreak of World War 1 in August 1914 created a split in the Irish Volunteers. John Redmond, in the interest of ensuring the enactment of the 'Home Rule Act', appealed for the Irish Volunteers to support the British and Allied war effort and to enlist in Irish regiments of the British army. Redmond's appeal caused a split in the organisation. A majority of 140,000 followed Redmond and formed the National Volunteers, who enlisted in Irish regiments of the

42 Creedon, Conal '1916 Rising Cork', Youtube, uploaded by Irishtown Productions, January 08, 2020, https://www.youtube.com/watch?v=X59c4egVjJI.

43 Creedon, Conal '1916 Rising Cork', Youtube, uploaded by Irishtown Productions, January 08, 2020, https://www.youtube.com/watch?v=X59c4egVjJI.

44 P.J. Murphy, B.M.H. witness statement, April 14, 1953. (N.A.1., B.M.H., WS 869), p. 5.

New British Army, while a minority of around 9,700 members remained as the original Irish Volunteers.[45] In Cork city all except a handful of volunteers, fewer than fifty, elected to follow Redmond. Following the split, the Volunteers in Cork established their new headquarters on Fisher Street, while the 'Irish National Volunteers' remained at the Corn Market headquarters.[46] It should be noted that the split in the Irish Volunteers had little effect on Na Fianna Éireann, neither nationally nor regionally in Cork city, with close to all Na Fianna members taking the side of the Irish Volunteers under Eoin MacNeill. Harrington (2016) writes that the reason for this was that Na Fianna was organised for a longer period than the Volunteers and so there was amongst its ranks a greater dedication to republican ideals, as opposed to the strong Redmondite constitutional nationalism present in the Volunteers. Na Fianna continued to forge strong relations with the Irish Volunteers after the split. Its initial role after the outbreak of the war was to organise against the British army recruitment drives as a pre-emptive action against the possibility of conscription being spread to Ireland. By 1915, as conditions changed, Na Fianna's role changed significantly. In response to the growing militarisation of Irish society, Na Fianna shifted more towards becoming a military organisation.[47]

Liam O'Callaghan stated in his 1947 witness statement that "Fianna leaders were later the pioneers in forming Volunteer companies…Up to 1915 the Fianna in Cork was purely a Scout movement. After that it became more of a military body and a training ground for the volunteers. We were getting some small arms, which the boys were picking up themselves, and the older boys were given training with the revolver. We also got some rook rifles".[48]

---

45 Cambell, Fergus (2005), 'Land and Revolution: Nationalist Politics in the West of Ireland, 1891–1921', p. 196.
46 P.J. Murphy, B.M.H. witness statement, April 14, 1953. (N.A.1., B.M.H., WS 869), p. 6.
47 'HE HISTORY OF NA FIANNA ÉIREANN IN CORK CITY 1910-1924' https://FiannaÉireannhistory.wordpress.com/2016/10/06/the-history-of-na-Fianna-Éireann-in-cork-city-1910-1924/, accessed June 22, 2022.
48 Seán Healy & Liam O'Callaghan, B.M.H. witness statement, October 04, 1947. (N.A.I., B.M.H, WS 47), p. 4.

CHAPTER FOUR

Na Fianna Éireann in Cork city and The Easter Rising (1916)

The historian Marnie Hay writes that from summer 1915 to spring 1916, many Fianna members across the country felt that the organisation, along with the IRB and the Irish Volunteers, was "moving rapidly towards a climax, which as it turned out, was the Easter Rising".[49] For the Cork city Fianna, firing practice with small arms had increased and some of the older boys had been given revolvers for personal use. Ammunition had been moved throughout the city by Na Fianna in the week before the Easter Rising. During Holy Week 1916, the Volunteers Cork city Battalion O/C, Seán O'Sullivan, had ordered Seámus Courtney (Captain, Na Fianna, Cork city) and Seán Healy (First Lieutenant, Na Fianna) to mobilise all of the more senior boys at the hall on Sheares Street for Easter Sunday morning: "we were armed with two or three rook rifles and eight or ten revolvers, some .22 and some .32. Seán Healy had a Lee Metford rifle and a good supply of .303".[50] In his witness statement taken in 1957, James Allan Busby recalled of the day that: "we paraded in Sheares Street with the Volunteers, and together with twelve other Fianna boys we marched with the Volunteer contingent to Capwell railway station, Cork, where we took the train to Crookstown in West Cork. From Crookstown we marched to Macroom. On reaching Macroom we were addressed by Seán O'Sullivan, the Volunteer Commandant".[51] All those

49 Hay, Marnie, 'The foundation and development of Na Fianna Éireann, 1909-16', Irish Historical Studies, xxxvi, no. 141 (May 2008), p. 68.

50 Seán Healy & Liam O'Callaghan, B.M.H. witness statement, October 04, 1947. (N.A.I., B.M.H, WS 47), p. 4.

51 James Allan Busby, B.M.H. witness statement, June 06, 1957. (N.A.I., B.M.H, WS 1628), p. 3.

present were informed by O'Sullivan that the parade was cancelled at which they returned to Cork city by train that evening (Appendix 1 - list of confirmed members of Cork city Fianna Éireann who marched with Volunteers from Crookstown to Macroom on Sunday 23 April 1916).

According to Busby's account of the following morning, Easter Monday, he along with other senior Fianna boys reported again to Sheares Street, where "I was given a double-barrelled shotgun and told to take up guard duty between the two roofs of the volunteers hall".[52] P.J. Murphy recalled that on Easter Monday both Tomás Mac Curtain and Terence MacSwiney were present at Sheares Street. A stand-to order was issued, sentries were posted, and defence preparations were made for the hall. Murphy himself was tasked along with other Fianna to report on military activity at the railway and Victoria military barracks.[53] James Allan Busby further stated that the senior Na Fianna boys were "in and out of the hall in Sheares St. all Easter week, night and day, but we received no instruction...a few volunteers and Fianna left Cork on bikes to go to Dublin and join in the fighting".[54] In the book 'Rebel Cork's Fighting Story 1916-1921' (1947), it records that Cork, like most of the rest of Ireland outside of Dublin, suffered from a confusion of contradictory orders issued from Volunteer headquarters during Easter week and as such the planned contribution of the Cork republicans to the insurrection failed to materialise. In the aftermath a subsequent inquiry absolved the Cork leaders from any blame.[55] On the Wednesday of Easter week an agreement had been reached between Dr Daniel Cohalan, the Auxiliary Bishop of Cork, with Mac Curtain, MacSwiney and the British military authorities. The Volunteers would give up their guns from Sheares Street to be stored in Lord Mayor Butterfield's storage room in the South Mall in the City. Busby stated that a number of volunteers refused to do this and that no member of Na Fianna gave up his weapons. Shortly after the Volunteers had deposited their rifles, British Army troops carried out a raid and all the deposited rifles were confiscated.

---

52 Ibid, p. 4.
53 P.J. Murphy, B.M.H. witness statement, April 14, 1953. (N.A.I., B.M.H., WS 869), p. 13.
54 James Allan Busby, B.M.H. witness statement, June 06, 1957. (N.A.I., B.M.H, WS 1628), p. 4.
55 O'Conchubhair, Brian (Series Editor), 'Rebel Cork's Fighting Story 1916-1921' (2009), Mercier Press, p. 31.

Simultaneously, another raiding party on Sheares Street led by the RIC arrested all the Volunteer officers present.[56] These officers were subsequently deported to British prisons.[57]

Seán Healy recounted in his 1947 witness statement how after Easter Week, the Cork Fianna "did everything possible to revive the spirit of the people and to change their apathetic attitude".[58] When Volunteers returned to Cork city from British prisons, the Fianna marched to meet them. This often caused some violent conflicts with the RIC, with baton charges against the crowd being used as a tactic. When the charges were unsuccessful the RIC used their carbines to clear the crowds. In one instance P.J. Murphy shot and wounded an RIC officer. Murphy stated in his 1953 witness statement that: "I used a .22 revolver and a policeman named Brown was slightly wounded on the temple".[59] This was in direct contradiction with the standing order for the boys not to use weapons without express permission. Murphy was called to an inquiry before the Volunteer Council and reprimanded for endangering life and was consequently temporarily stripped of his Cork city Slua command. As Murphy was leaving the room, Tomás Mac Curtain (who was presiding and was silent up to this point), "stood up and gave me a clap in the back saying I wish we could get the same spirit into the Volunteers".[60]

Later in 1916 after Seámus Courtney was released from prison, he and Seán Healy organised a concert in the City Hall to raise morale. Countess Markievicz was in attendance. Seán Healy recounted, "We asked Birdie Conway to sing 'The Wearing of the Green'...Liam O'Callaghan marched on to the stage carrying a green flag with harp and escorted by a guard of honour…with rifles and bayonets at the

---

56 P.J. Murphy, B.M.H. witness statement, April 14, 1953. (N.A.1., B.M.H., WS 869), pp. 14-15.

57 'THE HISTORY OF NA FIANNA ÉIREANN IN CORK CITY 1910-1924' https://FiannaÉireannhistory.wordpress.com/2016/10/06/the-history-of-na-Fianna-Éireann-in-cork-city-1910-1924/, accessed June 22, 2022.

58 Seán Healy & Liam O'Callaghan, B.M.H. witness statement, October 04, 1947. (N.A.I., B.M.H, WS 47), p. 5.

59 P.J. Murphy, B.M.H. witness statement, April 14, 1953. (N.A.1., B.M.H., WS 869), p. 16.

60 Ibid, p. 17.

slope, and in full uniform. The people went absolutely mad with enthusiasm…
We were very proud of the success of the concert at that particular time". [61]

Seámus Courtney
(Photo – January 22, 1916, Officers Training Camp at
Volunteers Hall, Sheares Street, Cork city)

---

61 Seán Healy & Liam O'Callaghan, B.M.H. witness statement, October 04, 1947. (N.A.I., B.M.H, WS 47), p. 5.

CHAPTER FIVE

The Impact of The Easter Rising: Na Fianna Éireann in Cork city (1917 – 1918)

The British Prime Minister Asquith did not foresee the public reaction in Ireland to the secret trials, hasty executions of leaders, and the large-scale deportation of those involved in the Easter Rising. By June 1916, many Irish people were showing sympathy towards the rebels and their families: "there were large attendances at commemorative masses and religious ceremonies, which became nothing more than large-scale displays of anti-British feeling".[62] The Catholic Bishop of Limerick, 'Edward O'Dwyer', expressed the public sentiment in his letter of 17 May 1916, to General John Maxwell (military governor for Ireland), saying, "I regard your action with horror, and I believe that it has outraged the conscience of the country".[63] On 7 December 1916, Lloyd George succeeded Asquith as the British Prime Minister and one of his first acts was to release the 600 Irish political prisoners interned in Britain since the rebellion. The release of these prisoners became the occasion for great public demonstrations in Ireland. The internment camps such as Frongoch where many Irish prisoners were held, have often been referred to during this time as "schools of Irish militant nationalism".[64] The released internees returning to Ireland in 1917 were anxious to prove their worth by continuing the struggle for Irish independence, "When the leaders

---

62 Tierney, Mark (1987), 'Ireland since 1870', C J Fallon, pp. 194-195.
63 Ibid, p. 194.
64 Ibid, p. 201.

began to reorganise in 1917, a new spirit was stirring in the people, and amongst the Volunteers its keynote was a determination to renew the conflict which had gone down in fire and death in Dublin".[65] Over the course of 1917, organisation both for the Volunteers and Na Fianna in Cork was steadily improved. James Busby estimated that in 1917 the Cork city Fianna had approximately 80 boys registered as members and the Cork leadership decided to expand to form two sluas in the city, "one catering for boys on the north side of the river Lee, and one on the south side".[66] George Hurley, another Cork city Fianna, elaborated in his witness statement in 1957 that the boundaries for the city's north side slua was from Mayfield to Clougheen; and for the south side it was from Blackrock to Dennehy's Cross.[67] The main activities of the Cork city Fianna in 1917 consisted of military drills, route-marching, scouting practice and revolver practice. The year 1917 saw frequent arrests and hunger strikes in Cork, while the Volunteers Hall in Sheares Street was forcibly closed by the military authorities.[68]

On the occasion of hunger strikes by Volunteer and Na Fianna prisoners held in Cork Gaol, Na Fianna boys from the city would take food and clothing to the prisoners in the gaol who were on remand and not on hunger strike. In March 1917 a meeting of Na Fianna and Volunteer officers at Sheares Street was raided by the police which resulted in the arrest and imprisonment of two Cork senior Fianna Seámus Courtney and Seán Healy. They were both charged with illegal drilling at the hall in Sheares Street and served three months in harsh conditions in Cork Gaol before their eventual release.[69]

The main efforts of the city's Volunteer battalions at this time were concentrated on training and on procuring arms. Senior members of Na Fianna were also employed in this task. P.J. Murphy – who at 15 was still a member of Na Fianna in 1917 – was tasked by Tomás Mac Curtain to contact soldiers in Cork barracks

---

65 O'Conchubhair, Brian (Series Editor), Rebel Cork's Fighting Story 1916-1921' (2009), Mercier Press, pp. 31-32.

66 James Allan Busby, B.M.H. witness statement, June 06, 1957. (N.A.I., B.M.H, WS 1628), p. 5.

67 George Hurley, B.M.H. witness statement, July 15, 1957. (N.A.I., B.M.H, WS 1630), p. 1.

68 O'Conchubhair, Brian (Series Editor), Rebel Cork's Fighting Story 1916-1921' (2009), Mercier Press, p. 32.

69 The History of Na Fianna Éireann – Seámus Courtney (1897-1918), https://FiannaÉireannhistory.wordpress.com/2014/08/09/seamus-courtney-1897-1918/, accessed June 23, 2022.

for the purchase of rifles "In one particular case a bread van was used in taking the rifles out of the barracks".[70] Murphy was also used by Mac Curtain as a contact for the purchase of revolvers from ex-soldiers: "Being a youth of 15 years I did not come under suspicion and was able to move around more freely than an adult".[71] One successful raid of that year carried out by Cork city Volunteers was on the Cork grammar school, which at the time was being used by the British military for training purposes: "a number of rifles and some equipment were secured".[72]

In October of 1917 another round-up of Cork Volunteer and senior Fianna officers took place. In total about 60 senior Republicans, including Na Fianna leader Seámus Courtney, were arrested. They all were sentenced to various terms of hard labour. Following sentencing, a meeting of the prisoners was held and it was decided to start a hunger strike. Four days later they were all released under the 'Cat and Mouse Act' which allowed for the early release of prisoners who were weakened by hunger striking.[73] By the end of spring 1918, Seámus Courtney's health had rapidly deteriorated. It was stated at the time that this was due to ill treatment he received, as well as the hard labour conditions during his two prison stays and his brief hunger strike in Cork Gaol.[74] To recuperate he went to stay with his aunt in Kerry, but passed away on 22 July 1918. He was only 21 years old. P.J. Murphy later stated of Na Fianna, "At the graveside we rendered military honours by firing three volleys with revolvers…This was the first time after Easter Week that firearms were used publicly, and it was the Fianna who gave the lead".[75]

In April 1918, the British parliament passed a Military Service Act, which empowered the government to extend conscription to Ireland. This led to the emergence of a nationwide anti-conscription campaign in Ireland. The anti-

---

70 P.J. Murphy, B.M.H. witness statement, April 14, 1953. (N.A.I., B.M.H., WS 869), p. 17.

71 Ibid, p.17.

72 O'Conchubhair, Brian (Series Editor), Rebel Cork's Fighting Story 1916-1921' (2009), Mercier Press, p. 32.

73 UK Parliament – 1913 Cat and Mouse Act, 'https://www.parliament.uk/about/living-heritage/transforming-society/electionsvoting/womenvote/case-study-the-right-to-vote/the-right-to-vote/winson-green-forcefeeding/cat-and-mouse-act/', Accessed June 23, 2022.

74 P.J. Murphy, B.M.H. witness statement, April 14, 1953. (N.A.I., B.M.H., WS 869), p. 17.

75 Ibid, p. 17.

conscription campaign caused alarm for the UK government, who realised that there were only 25,000 troops in Ireland, many of which were untrained men. George Hurley recalled "we attended recruiting meetings for the British army and created as much disturbance as possible. We distributed handbills advising men not to join the British army and helped generally in the type of activities suitable to boys".[76]

In the end the British government was forced to drop its plans for the imposition of conscription in Ireland.[77] In Cork city the threat of conscription led to an immediate swelling in the number of boys joining Na Fianna, with the number of members increasing from 80 to approximately 200.[78]

Following this, the Cork city Fianna was very active in the lead up to the general election of December 1918. Na Fianna boys distributed election material for Sinn Féin candidates, they carried out activities including posting bills, house to house collections for funds and general assistance in the intensive propaganda efforts put forward by Sinn Féin for that election.[79] The election was a significant success for republicanism, with Sinn Féin winning 73 out of 108 seats, and the first Dáil Éireann was formed and met for the first time in Mansion House, Dublin on January 21, 1919. The Dáil adopted three foundation deeds, of which the 'Declaration of Independence' was of the greatest importance to the IRA. This declared that a state of war existed that could never end until Ireland was definitively evacuated by the armed forces of Britain.[80]

---

76 George Hurley, B.M.H. witness statement, July 15, 1957. (N.A.I., B.M.H, WS 1630), p. 3.

77 Tierney, Mark (1987), 'Ireland since 1870', C J Fallon, pp. 209-210.

78 George Hurley, B.M.H. witness statement, July 15, 1957. (N.A.I., B.M.H, WS 1630), p. 1.

79 Charles Meaney, B.M.H. witness statement, July 15, 1957. (N.A.I., B.M.H, WS 1631), p. 1.

80 Townshend, Charles (1975), 'The British Campaign in Ireland, 1919-1921, The Development of Political and Military Policies, Oxford University Press, p. 15.

CHAPTER SIX

Na Fianna Éireann and The War of Independence in Cork city, 21 January 1919 – 11 July 1921

On 21 January 1919, the day Dáil Éireann held its first meeting in Dublin, the first shots of the Irish War of Independence were fired at Soloheadbeg, County Tipperary. Eight members of the South Tipperary Brigade of the Irish Volunteers attacked and shot dead two RIC constables.

In August 1919, the Volunteers changed their name to the 'Irish Republican Army' (IRA). Given the guerrilla tactics that would define this conflict, the IRA remained independent of the Dáil and ministerial control, with most IRA units operating under the control of local commanders. The Dáil was however obliged to endorse the military activities of the IRA and accept responsibility for its actions.[81]

In Cork County for the duration of the armed conflict, the Irish Volunteers (later to become the IRA) were organised into three brigades: The First Cork Brigade covered the centre of the county and stretched from the town of Youghal in the east to the border of County Kerry. The Second Cork Brigade covered North Cork and the Third Cork Brigade covered West Cork. The First Cork Brigade was the biggest brigade in the whole country, consisting of ten battalions. Initially the brigade was organised and led by Tomás Mac Curtain. Following his death, it was led by Terence MacSwiney and following his arrest (and subsequent

---

81 Tierney, Mark (1987), 'Ireland since 1870', C J Fallon, p. 222.

hunger strike and death) it was led by Seán O'Hegarty. Cork city was represented in the Cork First Brigade by two battalions, an active service unit and a special intelligence section. The core function of the Cork city Fianna during the war of independence years was to provide a supporting force for the two-city based First Brigade battalions.

The historian Gerard Murphy (2010) outlines three distinct phases to the Irish War of Independence in Cork. The first phase, he writes, ran from late 1919 to the early summer of 1920 and largely consisted of assassinations of RIC men by the IRA (note – the RIC was not an ordinary civil police force, but a military body, armed with rifles, bayonets, revolvers and batons). The second phase, which began in the summer of 1920, can be termed the 'Tan War'.

It saw the initial recruitment and entry of the special police reserve forces – known as the 'Black and Tans' and 'Auxiliaries' – into the conflict. The final phase ran from the beginning of 1921 to the truce that same year on 11 July. This period saw all of Munster under martial law.

The Martial Law Area (MLA) came under the control of the British army and the RIC, and the police reserve forces came under the army's control. Murphy has described the final phase in Cork as "by far the most violent, with both sides shooting civilians and carrying out unspeakable deeds on a daily basis".[82]

By early 1919 in Cork city, due to the increase in numbers following the conscription crisis, it was decided by the leadership to form a third slua in the city: "This was known as the centre sluagh and covered an area in the centre of the city extending from Custom House on the east to the Mardyke in the west. Frank McMahon was O/C of this sluagh".[83] Charles Meaney, Captain 'H Company', Cork city Fianna, stated in his military witness statement in 1957 that each slua contained an average of 30 to 40 boys. This number, however, he referred to as the 'paper' strength of the Fianna. Due to their youth, many of

---

82 Murphy, Gerard (2010), 'The Year of Disappearances – Political Killings in Cork 1921-1922', Gill & Macmillan, pp. 10-11.
83 George Hurley, B.M.H. witness statement, July 15, 1957. (N.A.I., B.M.H, WS 1630), p. 1.

the boys would not be called on for any hazardous tasks. From a pure military perspective, Meaney stated that "the really active members of the Fianna in Cork could be said to number not more than 30".[84]

In a letter dated July 09, 1942 from Honourable Secretary, Na Fianna Éireann, Denis Woods to M. Cummins, Office of the Defence, Military Services Pension Board, Woods outlines a summary of the military activities of the Cork city Fianna in support of the Cork city IRA battalions during the War of Independence: "The activities of Fianna in Cork were subject to the IRA Brigade Council and they were strictly confined to a series of activities which they (the Brigade) laid down for them, as it was considered that it was in their sphere they would usefully serve the cause. These outlined activities were intelligence such as observation of spies and suspected spies, observation of enemy posts and patrols, sorting and carrying orders for IRA ambush parties, storing arms, raids on enemy food supplies, raid for arms" (Appendix 2 – Denis Woods Letter of July 09, 1942).

In late 1920, an Active Service Unit (ASU) of the Cork city Fianna was formed. The Officer Commanding (O/C) for the ASU was Stephen Walsh. Former Fianna member George Hurley recalled in his military witness statement made in 1957 that "The unit consisted of about 20 to 30 of the more senior boys. About 12 of these were armed with revolvers when occasion demanded. This unit comprised Fianna from the IRA First Battalion area (north city) almost exclusively. It worked with the IRA men from the First Battalion".[85] Hurley stated that the main purpose of the ASU was to have Cork city senior Fianna boys available for any sudden call of duty from the First Battalion IRA (Note – Hurley stated that a smaller ASU was also formed on the south side of the city to support the IRA Second Battalion. That ASU was placed under the command of senior Fianna boy Frank Nolan).

By early 1921, the Cork city Fianna had formed a Brigade staff along with fifteen companies, of which eight companies were assigned to support the IRA

---

84 Charles Meaney, B.M.H. witness statement, June 11, 1957. (N.A.I., B.M.H, WS 1631), p. 2.
85 George Hurley, B.M.H. witness statement, July 15, 1957. (N.A.I., B.M.H, WS 1630), p. 2.

First Cork Brigade First Battalion and seven companies to support the IRA First Cork Brigade Second Battalion (Appendix 3 – MA/MSPC/FE/5, P. 33/60).

George Hurley listed the personnel at the time of the Truce as follows:

- **Cork city Fianna Brigade Staff:** O/C: Frank McMahon, Brigade Organiser and Vice O/C: Jack Carey, Adjutant: Dan Scully, Intelligence Officer: Michael O'Leary, O/C. City: Edward Gamble,

- **Cork city Fianna Battalions and Companies:**
  - **First Battalion:** O/C: Dan Mulroy, A/Company O/C: Stephen Walsh, B/Company O/C: Denis Woods, C/Company O/C: Con O'Leary, D/Company O/C: Stephen Wall and later Patrick Lynch, E/Company O/C: Leo Cahill, G/Company O/C: Daniel Gamble; H/Company O/C: Peter Young.

  - **Second Battalion:** O/C: Edward Murray, Adjutant: John Roynane, B/Company O/C: Richard O'Leary, C/Company O/C: William Quirke, D/Company O/C: Seán Downey, E/Company O/C: Frank Nolan, F/Company O/C: Christopher Hurley, G/Company O/C: Richard Noonan, H/Company O/C: Charles Meaney.[86]

Dan Scully, Cork city Fianna Adjutant (furthest right). Photo taken circa 1921.

---

86 George Hurley, B.M.H. witness statement, July 15, 1957. (N.A.I., B.M.H, WS 1630), p. 5.

In his 1957 military witness statement, Charles Meaney recalls the major Cork city Fianna activities as: (1) raids on private houses for arms, (2) scout duty for the IRA, (3) destruction of enemy stores, (4) enforcement of Belfast boycott, (5) attacks on individual enemy personnel, (6) carrying of dispatches and the transportation and storage of arms for the IRA First Cork Brigade.[87]

(1) Raids for arms:

Edward Horgan, First Lieutenant, H Company, IRA First Battalion, First Cork Brigade, stated in his witness statement on 26 June 1957, that in 1919 the Cork city IRA arms situation consisted of "a few revolvers and shotguns".[88] To improve this general situation an intensified effort was adopted across the First Cork Brigade area to procure arms. Brigade leadership issued orders to all companies to undertake the raiding of private houses in their districts where intelligence believed guns or ammunition may be held. Horgan stated the owners of these houses were "in practically every instance, of the so-called gentry class. They were all pro-British in their sympathies and many were ex-officers of the British Army".[89] Numerous instances occurred where senior Fianna boys actively took part in these raiding parties in conjunction with Cork city IRA members. Charles Meaney, Captain H Company (Cork city), Fianna, personally recalls taking part in two such raids, one on the house of a retired British army colonel in Douglas on 7 March 1920 and another on the house of an ex British Army Major named Gubbins in Dunkettle: "Three or four of us usually carried out these raids, one of us being armed with a revolver.…we found a few sporting guns, gunpowder, bandoliers, field-glasses, an officer's uniform and Sam Browne belts".[90] It should be noted concerning the carrying of arms that a distinct division did exist between the members of the IRA and Na Fianna Éireann in Cork city. George Hurley stated of Na Fianna: "Comparatively few members had guns of any kind. The more senior boys did have revolvers, but to the best of my recollection, there were

---

87 Ibid, p. 3
88 Edward Horgan, B.M.H. witness statement, June 26, 1957. (N.A.I., B.M.H, WS 1644), p. 3.
89 Ibid, p. 3
90 Charles Meaney, B.M.H. witness statement, July 15, 1957. (N.A.I., B.M.H, WS 1631), p. 3.

no more than a dozen revolvers in the hands of the Fianna during the period 1917-1921…a direction was given to the Fianna by IRA headquarters in Cork in 1920, that the Fianna was not to carry out any attacks on enemy forces by shooting, unless with the prior permission of the IRA. This instruction was, in the main, carried out, and, except for isolated (individual) cases, no organised armed attack was carried out on the enemy forces in Cork city by the Fianna".[91] Charles Meaney outlines that despite the difference on policy on the carrying and using of arms that the Cork city Fianna and IRA companies consistently acted in "close co-operation".[92]

In addition to the raids of private houses, Na Fianna Honourable Secretary Denis Woods, in his notes compiled in the 1930s for the support of former Cork city Fianna members in their IRA pension application process, records the following raids for arms and equipment and activities during the period April 1920 to March 1921. These were either independently led operations of the Cork city Fianna or in collaboration with members of the IRA First Battalion.

(Note – use of the circle bullet points as per listed below denote direct quotes from Denis Woods' private material).

- (IRA Collaboration) Armed raid on the Baden Powell rooms South Mall seized dummy rifles, bayonets, and equipment (raided several times) (P.Lynch, E.Gamble, C.Curtain, W.Quirke, D.Gamble, C.Woods, S.Walsh, D.Scully, E.Murray, J.Pierce, M.O'Leary, C.Herlihy),

- (IRA Collaboration) Armed Raid on Shines College Road – Result 1 Shot Gun (Armed – F.Nolan, W.Ross, T.Donovan, C. Meaney, J.Fennell, R.Mahoney, W.Quirke, J.Cummans)

- (IRA Collaboration) Raid on Rifle Range – Glen, Cork Barracks, Result 90 Rounds Ammunition (Armed – S.Walsh and 2 others unnamed)

---

91 George Hurley, B.M.H. witness statement, July 15, 1957. (N.A.I., B.M.H, WS 1630), p. 2.
92 Charles Meaney, B.M.H. witness statement, July 15, 1957. (N.A.I., B.M.H, WS 1631), p. 2.

- Raid on Tract shop – a number of important and useful books were seized including military training books (armed - E.Gamble, D.Scully and E.Murray, unarmed – L.Cahill, D.Mulroy, S.Wall),

- Removal of explosives from Andy Aherns on Grattan Street to Rathmore Terrace, (L.Clay, J.Peirce, E.Keating, M.O'Leary, E.Gamble, D.Gamble, D.Scully, E.Denny, C.O'Brien and S.Walsh).

(2) Scout duty for the IRA:

Charles Meaney stated of this duty during his time with the Cork city Fianna that "Many times we were called on to act as scouts for IRA units waiting in ambush. Our job was to give warning of the approach of enemy forces".[93] Meaney also categorises the following activities as falling under Scout duties: "Military and police barracks were watched and movements of troops, Black and Tans and RIC duly reported to the IRA. Suspected spies were followed by us and their activity reported on".[94] George Hurley also recalled this duty of the Cork Fianna: "Scouting duty for the IRA was of frequent occurrence, suspected spies were tracked and their movements reported to the IRA.".[95]

The notes compiled by Denis Woods in the 1930s classify this latter activity as 'Intelligence Work (IO)'. The details of 'IO' work conducted by senior members of Cork city Fianna during the period March 1920 to July 1921 include:

- Keeping Tans under observation in public house on South Main Street (D.Scully, J.Carey, C O'Brien, D.Gamble, M. O'Leary)

- Scouting and mobilising for IRA (J.Foley)

- IO Work on Herd (E.Warren)

- IO Work on Madden (W Rose, T.Donovan, R.Mahoney)

- IO Work on Murphy (T Donovan, W Rose, R.Mahoney)

---

93 Ibid, p. 4.
94 Ibid, p. 5.
95 George Hurley, B.M.H. witness statement, July 15, 1957. (N.A.I., B.M.H, WS 1630), p. 3.

- IO Work on Linehan (T.Barrett, D.Scully, M.Leary, E.Gamble, S.Wall and P. Lynch)

- IO Work on Hoare (T.Barrett)

- IO Work on McGiff (D.Scully, W.Quirke, E.Murray, D.Gamble)

- IO Work on Sullivan (T.Donovan and W.Rose) - "William Sullivan, Ex-Soldier, Place of Death – Tory Top Road, 14/02/21"[96]

- IO Work on Poland (E.Gamble, L.Cahill, D.Scully, D.Gamble, T.Twomey)

- IO Work on Good (E.Murray, E.Gamble, J.Peirce, J.Carey, D.Scully, D.Gamble and M.O'Leary). (Author's note: "John Good, Friar Street was identified as a spy by the IRA and shot. However, he survived the attack near the Labour Exchange where he worked. While the IRA believed that they had killed him he subsequently claimed compensation in 1921").[97]

- IO Work on Casey (Gratton Street) (E.Gamble, C.O'Brien, D.Woods, D.Gamble, J.Peirce)

- IO Work on D.Donovan (Shot) (E.Gamble, D.Gamble, M.O'Leary, S.Wall, D.Scully, T.Cahill and C.Curtain). "Denis Donovan, Ex-Soldier, Place of Death – Found at Ballygarvan, 12/04/21".[98] (Author's note: "Leo Buckley, staff officer for intelligence in the First Battalion of the First Cork Brigade, explained... By April 1921, Donovan had become a marked man. He 'was shot as a spy on brigade instructions. He was shot in Ballygarvan on 14th April 1921 [incorrect date], and a label "spies and informers beware" placed on his chest.' See Leo Buckley's WS 1714, 7, 12 (BMH))".[99]

---

96 Murphy, Gerard (2010), 'The Year of Disappearances – Political Killings in Cork 1921-1922', Gill & Macmillan, p. 41

97 Keane, Barry (15 February 2015) 'Final list file Shooting Incidents War of Independence Cork Ireland 1917-1921 Version 2', p. 10.

98 Murphy, Gerard (2010), 'The Year of Disappearances – Political Killings in Cork 1921-1922', Gill & Macmillan, p. 41.

99 'The Irish Revolution Project' https://www.ucc.ie/en/theirishrevolution/collections/cork-fatality-register/register-index/1921-188/, accessed: July 05, 2022.

- IO Work on Sherlock (Shot) (E.Gamble) - "21 May 1921, Sherlock shot but not killed"[100]

- IO Work on Begley (S.Walsh, D.Scully, D.Gamble, R.Flynn, M.O'Leary, E.Gamble) – (Author's note: "On July 11th at 11.55pm we captured Begley, a spy for whom we were on the look-out. He was executed on Saturday 16th".[101] According to a letter from the Department of Defence of the Irish Free State Government to John Begley's mother in November 1922 "As far as I can ascertain [he was] shot unofficially as a spy. I have not been able to trace his burial place").[102]

- IO Work on Farrell and Podesta (D. Scully, S.Wall, P.Lynch, L.Cahill, E.Gamble, D.Woods and D.Gamble). Additional notes of this operation compiled by Denis Woods state: Under orders awaiting arrest of suspects Farrell and Podesta at Blackpool during curfew – D.Woods (armed), J.Foley (armed), D.O'Mahoney, S.Wall (armed) and R.Flynn (armed), Sent to Tivoli with instructions to waylay Farrell and Podesta and shoot them – S.Walsh, P.Lynch, T.Forde (all armed). (Author's note: Further information on this operation is also outlined in the 'Guide to Military Service (1916-1923) Pensions Collection' by author Catriona Crowe: "The Fianna were instructed 'to waylay' two ex-servicemen named Farrell and Podesta in Tivoli 'and shoot them'. Podesta, a Protestant and a passionate loyalist invalided out of the army suffering from gas poisoning during the First World War, may or may not have been an informer in Cork in 1920… Podesta, whom the Cork IRA had in their sights but eventually decided not to kill, did become a significant though highly ineffective and insecure agent for the British intelligence agency MI6 in Dublin from 1940 to 1945").[103]

---

100 Keane, Barry (15 February 2015) 'Final list file Shooting Incidents War of Independence Cork Ireland 1917-1921 Version 2', p. 13.

101 Activity Reports of First and 6th Battalions Cork First Brigade for July 1921, Mulcahy, P/7/A/23.

102 Begley Correspondence in Department of Defence Series, A/07360

103 Crowe, Catriona (2012), 'Guide to the Military Service (1916-1923) Pensions Collection', Defence Forces.

(3) Destruction of Enemy Stores:

Both Charles Meaney and George Hurley recall in their military witness statements how Na Fianna frequently held up and destroyed provisions and various other goods and stores being transported from shops to the British military and RIC barracks in the city. Meaney recalls the hold up of a lorry with provisions in Alford Street: "when the lorry was loaded, we got on to it and drove it to Hardwick Street, where we emptied the contents (jam and other provisions) into a store. The stuff was later distributed to the relatives of men in gaol".[104]

The notes of Denis Woods also provide reference to these activities:

- Continuous raids on food supplies intended for RIC barracks the raids were carried out on the shops or on the vans: Names of the shops – Hogan's on Castle Street, O'Sullivan on Paul Street, Baltimore Stores on McCurtain Street, Barry on Douglas Street, Lunhams on White Street, O'Sullivan's on Oliver Plunkett Street, Buckley on Oliver Plunkett Street, Collins on Castle Street. (On Raids – T. Barrett, J. Murray, T. Murray, J. O'Sullivan, E. Hegarty)

- Date unnamed - Holding up laundry van on Brian Boru Bridge on the way to RIC. Barracks – J.Foley (armed) and D.O'Mahoney

- Date unnamed - Holding up lines men taking apparatus off them Watercourse Road and Commons road – D.Mulroy (armed), J.Foley, S.Wall (armed)

- Date unnamed - Dislocating telephone service – (continuous) – D.Mulroy (armed), T.Donovan (armed), J.Murray, W.Dennehy, L.Cahill (armed), S.Wall (armed), E.Gamble (armed) and W.Rose (armed).

(4) Enforcement of the Belfast Boycott:

In August 1920, Dáil Éireann ordered a boycott of goods from Belfast by shopkeepers throughout Ireland. This was in reaction to the expulsions of mainly Catholic workers from the Belfast shipyards and other places of work, as well as sectarian violence in the north of Ireland during the summer of 1920. According to George Hurley, "The Fianna was particularly active in enforcing the boycott of Belfast

104 Charles Meaney, B.M.H. witness statement, July 15, 1957. (N.A.I., B.M.H, WS 1631), p. 5.

goods being sold in shops. Daylight raids were of frequent occurrence; goods were removed from shops and the owners warned that the practice of selling such goods should stop. The measures taken by the Fianna in this respect were very effective in 'tightening' the boycott campaign in Cork city".[105] Charles Meaney recalled how Na Fianna boys visited many shops suspected of stocking goods from Belfast, the boys examined the invoices for date of purchase and the proprietors were warned not to sell the goods from Belfast. Meaney stated in the case of his company "it was seldom we removed any goods from shops, as the invoices in most cases showed that the goods had been in stock before the boycott order was made".[106]

The notes of Denis Woods provide numerous examples of Na Fianna raids for boycott goods during the period:

- Raids on Lester's chemist for boycott goods (P.Lynch, S.Walsh and R.Flynn – all armed)

- Raids on the city shops for Gallagher's cigarettes and boycott goods on several occasions (Armed – E.Gamble, P.Lynch, D.Woods, S.Walsh, D.Scully, S.Wall; Unarmed – L.Cahill and R.Flynn)

- Raid on Blair's Chemist for Boycott Goods (Armed – S.Walsh, S.Wall, D.Woods, E.Gamble, R.Flynn)

- Raid on Mayne's Chemist for Boycott goods (Armed – S.Wall, R.Flynn, J.Murray and S.Walsh)

- Raid on Fielding's Patrick Street for Boycott Goods (raided at least twice) (Armed – S.Wall, S.Walsh, D.Scully, D.Woods, P.Lynch, E.Gamble, R.Flynn; Unarmed – G.Hurley and C.Curtain)

- Raid on the Railway for boycott goods (threads) (Armed – P.Lynch and S.Walsh)

---

105 George Hurley, B.M.H. witness statement, July 15, 1957. (N.A.I., B.M.H, WS 1630), p. 3.
106 Charles Meaney, B.M.H. witness statement, June 11, 1957. (N.A.I., B.M.H, WS 1631), p. 6.

(5) Attacks on Individual Military Personnel:

Charles Meaney recalled in his 1957 witness statement that "Three or four of us waylaid soldiers and Black and Tans who were sometimes in the company of girls, or perhaps, leaving a public house in a drunken condition. Whenever the opportunity offered, we attacked then, took their equipment and, in quite a good few of instances got revolvers as well".[107] Meaney recalls a specific incident involving a group of off-duty unarmed soldiers and himself, Frank Nolan and two other Fianna members in which arms were discharged on Wellington Road: "we waded into them, beat them up and took their bandoliers…Nolan and I were armed with revolvers. We took cover and, as the soldiers approached, opened fire. They beat a hasty retreat. Next day we learned that one of the soldiers had been wounded in the neck".[108] George Hurley also recalled these types of instances: "on several occasions, our lads held up individual soldiers or Black and Tans and took their equipment".[109]

The pension application notes complied by Denis Woods list the following occurrences:

- Holding up soldiers and taking equipment off them (C.Curtain, C.Meaney and S.Wall),

- Armed attack on soldiers' result – wounding one on Wellington Road, (Armed – C.Meaney, C.Curtain, F.Nolan, W.Rose),

- Armed attack on Tan wounding him at South Main Street (E.Gamble and C.O'Brien)

- Burning military car outside courthouse (E.Gamble, J.O'Sullivan, E.Keating and C.O'Brien – (Burned by Jo Mahony and Keating – G Company)

- Raid for arms holding up ex-soldiers at St Mary's Hall and taking revolvers off them (S.Walsh and P.Lynch),

---

107 Ibid, p.6.

108 Ibid, p.7.

109 George Hurley, B.M.H. witness statement, July 15, 1957. (N.A.I., B.M.H, WS 1630), p. 3.

- Raid for arms taking revolver off suspect (Sullivan) at Pine Street (Armed – S.Walsh, J.Carey, E.Gamble, P.Lynch, non-armed – D.Gamble and R.Flynn),

- Arresting and Conveying suspects believed to have arms to Cork Park and interrogating them (Armed – S.Walsh, D.Woods, R.Flynn, P.Lynch and S.Wall),

- Removing arms from Fair Hill to CAFÉ NA CUIN and back again for IRA A.S.U. (Jim O'Leary Hall and Washington Street) (T.Barrett),

- Disarming Black and Tan at Court House (obtained a revolver) (Armed – S.Walsh, Unarmed – J.Carey, M.O'Leary),

- Disarming Black and Tan at Kyrls Quay (revolver) (Armed – E.Gamble, S.Walsh, unarmed – D.Gamble, P.Lynch, G.Hurley, E.Keating, L.Clay),

- Disarming Black and Tan at Maylor Street (revolver) (Armed – S.Walsh, unarmed – E.Gamble, J.Carey, P.Lynch, E.Keating).

- Reprisals for Dripsey Ambush scouting – S.Walsh and E.Gamble (both armed)

(Author's note: Edward Horgan in his military witness statement taken in June 1957 referred to this incident. In February 1921, following an IRA ambush of Black and Tans at the village of Dripsey in County Cork, a number of IRA prisoners were "brutally done to death by the 'Tans', an order was issued by the First Cork Brigade O/C that men from every company of the two Cork city battalions should patrol the streets under arms on the night of First March, 1921, and shoot every member of the British forces to be met with whether they were armed or not... Only one of these patrols met any of the enemy").[110] As per the notes compiled by Na Fianna Secretary, Denis Woods in the 1930s, both Stephen Walsh (O/C Na Fianna, First Battalion, A Company) and Edward Murray (O/C Na Fianna, Second Battalion) were the Cork city Fianna members who were ordered on armed patrol.

---

110 Edward Horgan, B.M.H. witness statement, June 26, 1957. (N.A.I., B.M.H, WS 1644), p. 11.

(6) Carrying of Despatches, Transportation and Storage of Arms:

According to Charles Meaney, the carrying of IRA dispatches was part of routine work conducted by Na Fianna, often in co-operation with the Cork city branch of Cumann na mBan. John Watts in his 1981 PhD thesis 'Na Fianna Éireann: A Case Study of a Political Youth Organisation' outlined how the carrying of despatches was assigned as the main task of Na Fianna juniors as it was thought by the IRA leadership that they made the least conspicuous messengers.[111] This was also why Na Fianna members were frequently involved in the removal and transportation of arms. Former Cork Fianna John Murray in his 1979 interview with John Watts (per Watts notes) recalled, "it was their unobtrusiveness, in fact, that determined the kind of support duties assigned to the younger Fianna. Despatches could be easily hidden inside a bicycle frame and enemy communications effectively blocked by cutting telegraph wires or digging trenches in familiar country roads. Boys could stand unchallenged at cross-roads with horse and trap, carry weapons to rendezvous in relative safety, and, as they had always done, distribute literature, paste up and tear down posters, steward republican meetings and heckle those of their opponents. Fiannaí were especially useful in bringing explosives into Cork city centre which because it is surrounded by two branches of the river and is only accessible by bridge, could easily be road-blocked by the authorities". According to Watts "as in all towns under Martial law, Fianna juniors played a particularly valuable part in maintaining supplies because persons under sixteen were allowed to come and go more readily than adults".[112]

The notes of Denis Woods provide numerous references to the involvement of the Cork city Fianna in the transportation and storage of arms:

- Date unnamed – Storing and Carrying arms for Fianna – J.O'Brien (21 Douglas Street)
- Special Duty at Sheares Street – E.Murray.

---

111 Watts, John R. (1981) 'Na Fianna Éireann: A Case Study of a Political Youth Organisation', University of Glasgow, p. 122.
112 Ibid, p. 160.

- Carried bombs to Washington street for G. Company Ambush Party (C.Curtain and E.Gamble) (Author's note: concerning this incident, members of the Cork city IRA active service unit were involved in a series of operations of taking up positions along routes frequently taken by the police and military. Patrick Murray, Officer in Command of C Company, First Battalion, IRA First Cork Brigade recalls in his witness statement made in 1953: "The unit's first ambush occurred on 12 April 1921, just after 10am, when bombs were thrown into a lorry in Washington Street at the junction with Little Anne Street. The bombs failed to explode, and the military returned fire wounding some civilians").[113]

- Holding arms for IRA (W.Dennehy, S.Wall, J.Foley, E.Gamble, D.Woods, D.Scully, T.Donovan)

- Removing of Company dump from Gamblers on Gratton Street to Coach Street (E.Gamble in charge, several members of Fianna engaged)

- Removing arms from T.O'Sullivan's (Brigade O.C. Fianna) - Douglas Street to Hibernian Buildings (E.Murray)

- Removing shot gun and ammunition from Adelaide Street to Grand Parade for IRA G.Company,

- Removal of ammunition and explosives from SS Elblana to Drinan Street (E.Gamble, J.O'Brien, P. Grant (B company IRA)),

- Removing arms and ammunition from F.Murray's house to North Main Street on 2 occasions (J.Murray)

- 16/05/1921 - making a dug out for dumping arms – L.Cahill, D.Mulroy, J.Foley, S.Wall and E.Hegarty (all armed).

- Housing armed party of IRA (B Company) at 42 Maylor street – D. Woods and D. Scully – "All members of Active Service Unit held arms". (Author's note: this event occurred on May 12, 1920, an armed Cork city IRA Party stayed overnight at 42 Maylor street in case of British military or police reprisals for the killings the previous day on May 11, 1920 at 10.30pm on the Lower

113 Patrick A. Murray, B.M.H. witness statement, February 26, 1957. (N.A.I., B.M.H, WS 1584), p. 22.

Glanmire Road of RIC Constables Garvey and Harrington who (following an IRA Council Inquest) were believed to have participated in the assassination of Lord Mayor Tomás Mac Curtain and they were then targeted in reprisal).

- Housing W.J. Barry – Foreman of Jury on Inquest of Thomas McCurtain – 42 Maylor Street (D.Scully and D.Woods) (Author's note: according to an article from The Cork Independent, Patrick O'Sullivan of Bantry and The Silver Key Public House, Ballinlough, noted: The official jury summoned by the RIC were evidently afraid to put in an appearance when the coroner called them together. Commandant Jerome O'Donovan then took the initiative and selected a republican jury. The inquest lasted three weeks and during that time we were constantly under the observation of the RIC until we were known by sight to every constable in the city).[114]

(7) Additional Cork city Fianna activities March 1920 - July 1921:
The destruction of mail vehicles: Charles Meaney recalled how in compliance with orders from IRA General Headquarters to destroy all military equipment and stores, the Cork city Fianna launched a burning campaign on the mail vehicles in the sheds near the General Post Office in Cork. Meaney stated how himself, Frank Nolan and six other Fianna boys "knew that some postmen came on duty at 6 a.m. and when they did come and had opened up the place, we went in after them and held them up. We sprinkled petrol over the lorries and over a number of three-wheeled bicycles with baskets attached. A lighted match was thrown on the lot and a terrific explosion occurred. All of us, including the postal officials, got safely away. The place was a blazing inferno and defied the efforts of the fire brigade for a long time to bring it under control. All the lorries were destroyed".[115]

The notes of Denis Woods also cite this burning incident and the names of those involved:

- Burning Mail baskets and 2 trucks (Baskets at GPO, Trucks at Phoenix Street)

---

114 Remembering 1920: The inquest jury speaks', https://www.corkindependent.com/2020/04/23/remembering-1920-the-inquest-jury-speaks/, accessed – July 05, 2022.
115 Charles Meaney, B.M.H. witness statement, June 11, 1957. (N.A.I., B.M.H, WS 1631), p. 8.

- (Armed – C.Meaney, F.Nolan, E.Murray, Unarmed – W.Rose, C.Curtain, W.Martin, T.Donovan, W.Quirke),

In addition to the above, the former Cork Fianna John Murray, when interviewed by John Watts as part of the research for his 1981 thesis, recalled an incident where Na Fianna "mounted a concerted operation in which every post office in town was raided on the one night and the stamps stolen".[116]

Theft of Loyalist Bicycles: Charles Meaney recalled in his witness statement how, on orders from the IRA leadership, Na Fianna members were instructed to steal bicycles from the houses of known loyalists in the city for the purpose of their use by IRA flying columns in Cork County. Meaney stated "About six of us took on this job and in one day's raiding we got upwards of 40 bicycles, including eight which we took from the Telephone Exchange in the South Mall (very near the County Club, a rendezvous for enemy officers). We took the bicycles to a shed in Sawmill St. where they were repainted to prevent identification by a man always there for that work". [117]

The notes of Denis Woods cite numerous instances of bicycle theft by Cork city Fianna:

- Continuous: Holding up loyalists for their cycles (Armed – F.Nolan, W.Rose, C.Meaney, T.Donovan, unarmed – R.Mahoney, J.Fennell)

- March 1920 to April 1921: Seizing of cycles from known Loyalists throughout the city (continuous for Fianna A.S.U – First and Second Battalions)

- 05/07/1920 – Soldiers' cycles taken at Western Road

- 12/05/1921 - Bicycles taken at Blackrock and Douglas

---

116 Watts, John R. (1981) 'Na Fianna Éireann: A Case Study of a Political Youth Organisation', University of Glasgow, p. 157.

117 Charles Meaney, B.M.H. witness statement, June 11, 1957. (N.A.I., B.M.H, WS 1631), p. 8.

The campaign against Anti-Republican newspapers: The former Cork city Fianna John Murray, when interviewed by John Watts for his 1981 PhD thesis, stated that particularly in the early stages of the War of Independence "when the people had not come down on the side of the Republican forces, it was essential to minimise the effects of pro-British propaganda. At stations, and especially at docksides, armed Fianna units regularly confiscated and destroyed newspapers as they arrived from Britain".[118] Murray recalled that Cork Fianna officers regularly boarded the steam-packet ships in Cork harbour and dumped the newspapers overboard. Murray recalled another operation when over forty Fianna officers under Frank McMahon raided the Cork Examiner's premises and its "presses were smashed".[119]

According to the Examiner's own archives, this incident occurred on 24 December 1920:

"A number of armed men, wearing masks or other disguises, who announced that they were acting under the orders of the Irish Republic, made a deliberate effort to fire with incendiary bombs the printing departments in Faulkner's Lane, and also hacked with sledgehammers or such heavy weapons the two rotary machines in the printing room, Bowling Green Street.

The damage done to three valuable printing machines is considerable. One, capable of printing a 16-page paper at a rate of over 20,000 per hour, is almost totally destroyed. This machine is situated under the compositing room. In the Bowling Green Street premises, there are two such large machines, one fitted to bring out a 16-page paper and the other a 24-page paper. Those two most up to date machines were pounded with heavy instruments and vital parts destroyed and there are indentations on heavy steel wheels, showing that violent force was employed". [120]

---

118 Watts, John R. (1981) 'Na Fianna Éireann: A Case Study of a Political Youth Organisation', University of Glasgow, p. 157.

119 Ibid, p.157.

120 'Christmas Eve, 1920: Armed men attack Examiner offices', https://www.irishexaminer.com/news/spotlight/arid-40196055.html, accessed July 05, 2022.

The notes of Denis Woods also refer to Na Fianna operations involving the theft and destruction of newspapers in Cork city:

- 23/05/1921 - Carload English papers taken at Bowling Green Street and destroyed.

- Date unnamed - Raid on the railway for Boycott Newspapers and commandeering the van, papers dumped in the river (Armed – S.Wall, S.Walsh, P.Lynch, D.Woods; Unarmed – D.Mulroy, R.Cremin and J.Murray)

- Date unnamed - Raids for Boycott newspapers waylaid vans at St Patricks Church and dumped them in the river (Armed – E.Gamble, D.Scully, D.Woods, R.Flynn, S.Wall, S.Walsh)

- Date unnamed - Raid on News Bros for Boycott Newspapers and dumped same in the river.

- Date unnamed – Na Fianna hand-painting posters at own house and posting up around city – T.Donovan, W.Rose, J.Fennell, R.Mahoney and M.Riordan

Na Fianna Regular Propaganda and IRA Support: As per the notes of Denis Woods:

- 1918-1919: Church Door Collections for Fianna Funds - Several arrested,

- 04/1918 – 03/1919: General election work, anniversary parades in the face of enemy proclamation, effacing enemy poster (proclamations). Obstructing RIC. and Military

- April 1920 – March 1921: Assisting Irish Republican Courts collecting fines and prisoners (General for Fianna A.S.U.)

- Date unnamed: Guarding prisoner (a civilian) at Blackrock Castle overnight (D.Woods and S.Wall)

- Date unnamed: Guarding prisoner at McGurks, North Main Street (P.Lynch, E.Gamble, D.Gamble, D.Scully and others)

CHAPTER SEVEN

The Relationship between Na Fianna Éireann in Cork city and the IRA First Cork Brigade, First and Second Battalions

Peter Hart (1998) wrote how in Cork the enemies of the IRA were struck by the extreme youth of its volunteers. Hart stated there was "a widely shared perception of Sinn Féin – and especially the Volunteers - as a youth movement".[121] The ages of IRA Volunteers in both Cork city and county during the years of the War of Independence show that between 1920 and 1921, for the general rank and file, 25% of the Volunteers were under the age of 20, while an additional 58% were between the ages of 20 and 29. In the case of IRA Officers in Cork during 1920-1921, 10% were under the age of 20, while an additional 60% of officers were between the ages of 20 and 29.[122] John Watts in his 1981 PhD thesis wrote how, in the year following the Easter Rising, senior Irish Volunteer representatives met with the newly appointed Fianna G.H.Q staff for discussions towards the eventual integration of the two forces.[123] The Volunteers' aim, even at this early stage, was to ensure that a regular flow would exist of trained recruits from Na Fianna into established Volunteer companies. In an effort to achieve this, it

121 Hart, Peter (1999), 'The I.R.A. & Its Enemies – Violence and Community in Cork 1916-1923', Clarendon Press, Oxford, p. 166.

122 Ibid, p. 171.

123 Watts, John R. (1981) 'Na Fianna Éireann: A Case Study of a Political Youth Organisation', University of Glasgow, p. 162.

was agreed to match the command structures of the two organisations. At the 1918 Ard Fheis, Na Fianna was reorganised on a Brigade level. The formation of Dáil Éireann in January 1919 "totally altered the status of the Volunteers and Fianna".[124] The Volunteers became the Army of the Irish Republic (IRA) under Dáil Éireann's Ministry of Defence. In addition, Na Fianna Éireann were declared as an official junior section of the Irish Republican Army, also under the control of the Ministry of Defence. At the 1919 Ard Fheis, Na Fianna Éireann members formally pledged their allegiance to Dáil Éireann. As the War of Independence progressed it was decided by senior leadership that a common military policy for both organisations needed to operate under a combined central authority. Hence "a composite council of Fianna and the IRA was set up by the Minister of Defence, Cathal Brugha, in December 1920, composed of three members of each G.H.Q staff with the minister or his nominee presiding".[125] The council established a practical partnership agreement, which was issued by memorandum to all Fianna companies by Na Fianna's Adjutant General. The memorandum stated that the Fianna would "assist the Volunteers in every manner possible, under its own officers, and though acting in cooperation would remain in most respects a separate organisation…Fianna's military role would normally be confined to giving assistance where required in joint operations in which its own commanding officers would themselves be answerable to Volunteer officers of equivalent rank. Independent operations by Fianna Active Service Units would require prior sanction by the local Army Battalion Commandant".[126]

In theory this memorandum outlined a sound strategic plan for an effective operational partnership between the two organisations across the country, however in reality the Fianna Adjutant General, Richard Mulcahy's report for the period ending 15/08/1921 outlined how the only locations where the terms of the memorandum were actually carried out were in the cities of Dublin, Cork and Belfast. Outside of these three areas, Mulcahy stated "the attitude adopted

---

124 Ibid, p. 162.
125 Ibid, p.163.
126 Ibid, p. 164.

by the I.V. (sic) towards the Fianna is one which is rather incomprehensible …
we have found that in most cases the I.V. have not made the slightest attempt to
avail themselves of the advantage of boys over men, and that the general opinion
is that the Fianna are only youngsters and should be treated like children".[127]

In Cork city, Na Fianna Éireann members were being effectively utilised by
the IRA First Cork Brigade in full compliance with the memorandum of Richard
Mulcahy. Indeed, John Watts has stated that in terms of graduation from the
ranks of Na Fianna to the IRA during the period 1920-1921, while Dublin had
a high level of approximately 50% of Fianna members transferred over, in Cork
this proportion was far higher. By contrast, in other areas of the country the
transfer rate was minimal: "in one Battalion in the West…which numbered 150
boys all ranks, only four graduated to the Volunteers before the Truce".[128] Peter
Hart (1998) also acknowledged this situation in Cork city during the war, in one
of only two references of Na Fianna in his 1998 work. He wrote "The rank and
file did retain a significant – albeit declining-proportion of teenagers, suggesting
a fairly consistent intake of new recruits. Many of these were graduates of the
Fianna, the republican boy scouts".[129] In the military witness statements of P.J.
Murphy and First Battalion, H Company, First Lieutenant, Edward Horgan both
men stated their republican service commenced with Na Fianna Éireann in Cork
city before each being transferred to the IRA First Cork Brigade in 1918.

Notable graduates of the Cork city Fianna to IRA active service include
Seámus Quirke, who was killed in County Galway by British auxiliaries on 9
September 1920 aged 23; and Christopher Lucey, who was shot dead by British
forces at Tureen Dubh, Ballingeary on 10 November 1920. Lucey was 22 at the
time of his death and had attained the rank of Section Commander with 'B'
Company, First Battalion, IRA, First Cork Brigade.

---

127 Ibid, p. 165.
128 Ibid, p. 166.
129 Hart, Peter (1999), 'The I.R.A. & Its Enemies – Violence and Community in Cork 1916-1923', Clarendon
Press, Oxford, p. 171.

Seámus Quirke, 1916 as a Lt. in the Cork city Fianna Éireann,

Christopher Lucey, 1916, Cork city Fianna Éireann

Richard Noonan, Officer Commanding, G Company, Second Battalion, Fianna, Cork city

Richard Noonan was an active member of Na Fianna Éireann in Cork city from first joining circa 1914 up to 1921 when he was transferred from his position as commanding officer of the Fianna Éireann, G Company, Cork city Second Battalion into the regular ranks of the IRA.

He served from 1921 to the time of the Truce with G Company, Second battalion, First Cork Brigade. He was active with the anti-Treaty IRA in Limerick after the outbreak of the Civil War and was arrested by Free State Army soldiers in August 1922 when he returned to Cork city for the funeral of his brother Thomas. Richard died as a Republican prisoner in Cork County Gaol on 11 October 1922 aged 18. The cause of his death was officially determined to be cardiac failure / heart disease. Noonan's Road in Cork city, where he lived, is named after him.

Richard Noonan was buried in the Republican Plot in St. Finbarr's Cemetery in Cork.

Peter Hart offered an explanation for the particularly close ties between the two organisations, suggesting that in Cork a male youth subculture had been formed in which participation in revolutionary activities was largely aligned with conformity with the group: "This youth subculture was a collective one, formed around long-lived groupings of brothers, cousins, neighbours, schoolmates, and the like who played, and often worked, together...A young man's status in the community depends to a great extent on being accepted by this group and by his full participation in its activities. Such cliques, and their territory, bands, and teams, were a very powerful focus for individual and collective identities and loyalties".[130]

An examination of Brigade membership (Appendix 4) of the Cork city Fianna from 1917 to 1921 tends to lend credence to Hart's theory. For example, the First and Second Lieutenants assigned to the First Battalion area during the period 1917 to 1918 were the stepbrothers Seán Scully and Christopher 'Chris' Woods. By 1919, both had been promoted to Captain Seán Scully and First Lieutenant Chris Woods. In the period 1919-1920, both Seán Scully and Chris Woods were transferred from Na Fianna Éireann to the IRA First Cork Brigade, while each of their younger brothers – Captain Daniel Scully and First Lieutenant Denis Woods – by 1921 had subsequently assumed their rank within the Cork city Fianna. Similarly, the brothers Edward and Daniel Gamble are also listed as both having served within the Cork city Fianna during the years 1919 to 1921. (Appendix 5 – Transcript of the sworn evidence interview given by the military service pension applicant Christopher Woods before the Pensions Advisory Committee, on May 30, 1939, detailing his service with the Cork city Fianna Éireann from 1916 to his progression from Na Fianna Éireann to the Cork city IRA and his eventual appointment to the rank of Intelligence Officer for B Company, First Battalion, First Cork Brigade in May 1921).

---

130 Hart, Peter (1999), 'The I.R.A. & Its Enemies – Violence and Community in Cork 1916-1923', Clarendon Press, Oxford, pp. 176-177.

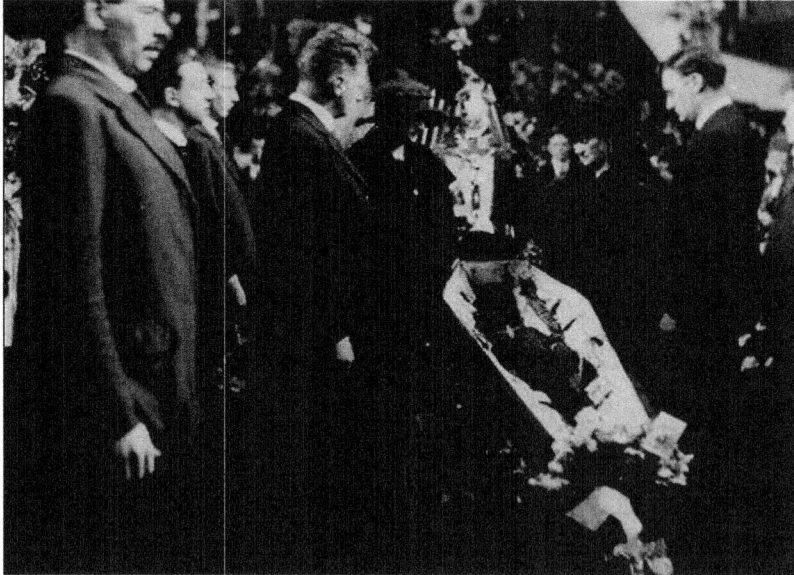

Above - Former Fianna (1917-1920) and IRA Volunteer (1920-1923) Christopher Woods (second from left) serving as one of the Republican guards over the remains of Lord Mayor of Cork, Terence MacSwiney, lying in state in Cork city on 31 October 1920.

Lord Mayor MacSwiney died age 41 on 25 October 1920, following his 74 days on hunger strike at HM Prison Brixton, London. Terence MacSwiney is buried in the Republican plot in Saint Finbarr's Cemetery in Cork city.

CHAPTER EIGHT

The Free State Recognition of Na Fianna Éireann Military Service in Cork city, from Easter 1916 to 11 July 1921

I n 1924, the Cumann na nGaedheal government of the Irish Free State introduced the first Military Service Pension (MSP) Act. This was limited in scope to pro-Treaty Civil War veterans with pre-Truce (1916 to 1921) military service. Ten years later, a Fianna Fáil government passed the Military Service Pensions Act, 1934, which allowed for applications from anti-Treaty Civil War veterans with pre-Truce service and War of Independence veterans whose service ended at the Truce. The 1934 Act was also extended to consider applications from women who served on the Cumann na mBan Executive from 1915 to 1922.

Eve Morrison writes that by 1957, less than 20% of the 82,000 pension applications had been approved by the Department of Defence.[131] According to Marie Coleman, the Irish military service pensions differed substantially from military pensions awarded by countries such as Spain or the United States in that "they were awarded for service in a conflict of relatively short duration, rather than on grounds of conflict-related disability or injury, or to dependants of combat fatalities".[132]

---

131 Morrison, Eve (2016) 'Chapter Eight - Witnessing the Republic: the Ernie O'Malley Notebook Interviews and the Bureau of Military History Compared', p.125, In 'Cormac K.H. O'Malley & John P. Waters (eds.), Modern Ireland and Revolution: Ernie O'Malley in Context', Dublin: Irish Academic Press.

132 Coleman, Marie, 'Military Service Pension for Veterans of the Irish Revolution, 1916-1923', War in History, April 2013, Vol. 20, No. 2 (April 2013), p. 202, Sage Publications Ltd.

Following the introduction of the 1934 Pension Act, the Department of Defence requested that old IRA, Cumann na mBan, Citizen Army, and Fianna Éireann veterans throughout Ireland set up advisory committees for the purpose of corroborating the military activities claimed in the pension applications of their former members. For this purpose, during the period 1934 to 1943, Denis Woods, in his role as Na Fianna Éireann's Honourable Secretary for the Cork region, compiled notes and advocated to the Office of the Department of Defence, Military Service Pension Board on behalf of his former Fianna comrades.

Eve Morrison states, "From 1935 until c 1945, these bodies compiled nominal rolls of members and activity reports for validating individual applications and nominated former officers to act as verifiers for pension applicants from their area".[133] Marie Coleman writes how the biggest problem in the decision process on pension applications was the absence of a definition of what constituted military 'Active Service': "a failing in the original act of 1924 that was not rectified in any of the subsequent legislation and that remained one of the greatest difficulties with the system throughout its existence".[134] As per Denis Woods' letter to M.Cummins, Office of the Department of Defence on 9 July 1942 (Appendix 2), by that date only two former officers of the Cork Fianna had been awarded a Military Pension under the 1934 Act.

The later decisions on the awarding of the class of Service (1917-1921) Medal to former Fianna members subsequently stemmed from whether they were awarded a Military Pension under the 1924 or 1934 Acts. On 26 May 1942 the Free State Government approved the recommendation of the Minister for Defence, Mr Oscar Traynor, T.D., that a Service (1917-1921) Medal with a Comrac Bar (indicating active military service, Comrac is the Irish for Struggle) should be issued to those applicants in possession of a military service certificate entitling them to a pension under the Military Service Pensions Acts, 1924 and 1934

---

133 Morrison, Eve (2016) 'Chapter Eight - Witnessing the Republic: the Ernie O'Malley Notebook Interviews and the Bureau of Military History Compared', p.134, In 'Cormac K.H. O'Malley & John P. Waters (eds.), Modern Ireland and Revolution: Ernie O'Malley in Context', Dublin: Irish Academic Press.

134 Coleman, Marie, 'Military Service Pension for Veterans of the Irish Revolution, 1916-1923', War in History, April 2013, Vol. 20, No. 2 (April 2013), p. 210, Sage Publications Ltd.

in respect of the period between 1916 and 11 July 1921. Those applicants who were not in possession of a military service certificate, but who could satisfy the Minister that had they applied for a pension – their service was such as would have merited the award of a pension – would also be issued the Service (1917-1921) Medal with a Comrac Bar.

Above - The Service (1917-1921) Medal with a Comrac Bar

This medal was issued to those who were deemed to have taken part in the War of Independence by engaging in active military service (involved in military operations). In total there were 15,224 Service Medals with a Comrac Bar issued. (Note: These figures include re-issued medals and therefore cannot be relied on to indicate the exact numbers who took part in the War of Independence). According to the Irish Military Archives online database, no Cork city member of Na Fianna Éireann at the time of the Truce was issued a Medal with a Comrac Bar (Note – this does not include former Fianna who had transferred over to membership of the IRA at least three months before the date of the Truce). In fact, in County Cork as a whole, only one former Fianna at the time of the Truce was awarded a Service Medal with a Comrac Bar. (Note – This was Robert Leahy, First Cork Brigade, 4th Battalion, Fianna A Company. The Medal with a Comrac Bar was issued in 1963. The applicant stated that he had been imprisoned in Parkhurst, Isle of Wight, in 1921. As per Irish Military Archives Medal File - MD11017).

Above - The Service (1917-1921) Medal Without a Comrac Bar

This medal was issued to persons whose service was not deemed to be active military service, but who were members of Óglaigh na hÉireann (Irish Republican Army), Fianna Éireann, Cumann na mBan or the Irish Citizen Army for the three months ended on the date of the Truce – 11 July 1921. In total 47,644 service medals without a Comrac Bar were issued. (Note – again these figures include re-issued medals and therefore cannot be relied on to indicate the numbers who took part in the War of Independence).[135]

According to the Irish Military Archives online database, 94 members of the First Cork Brigade, Fianna Éireann were awarded the Medal Without a Comrac Bar. Amongst these 94 medal recipients were a number of former senior Fianna Officers and members of the 1921 Fianna Active Service Unit in Cork city. These members include, amongst others, Edward Gamble, Denis Woods, James Allan Busby and James Wickham.

Marie Coleman writes that in 1955 the Department of Defence established a definition of 'Active Service': "any person who participated in an engagement against enemy forces, such participation being in the immediate area of operations and as an integral part of the operating force...They also had to have served in the most intense phases of the War of Independence between April 1920 and July 1921, and undertaken duties that included attacking the enemy, obstructing communications, acquiring and transporting arms and ammunition, guarding prisoners, attending training camps and battalion or brigade meetings, carrying despatches, providing first aid, and assisting volunteers on the run".[136]

Coleman states however that this definition of active service did not extend to members of Cumann na mBan or Na Fianna Éireann. No clarification on the rationale of the decision to limit the application of this definition was provided by the Department of Defence.

---

135 'The Irish War', https://www.theirishwar.com/product/comrac-bar-for-the-black-tan-medal-comrac-bar-19171921/, accessed July 10, 2022

136 Coleman, Marie, 'Military Service Pension for Veterans of the Irish Revolution, 1916-1923', War in History, April 2013, Vol. 20, No. 2 (April 2013), p. 211, Sage Publications Ltd.

CHAPTER NINE

The Murder of Cork city
Fianna Patrick Hanley

Both George Hurley and John Murray in their 1979 interviews with John Watts discuss the murder of Cork city Fianna Patrick Hanley, age 17. The incident occurred at approximately 11.45pm, on the night of 17 November 1920, at Hanley's mother's home at number 2 Broad Street. Hurley also discusses the death of Hanley in his military witness statement taken in July 1957. Hurley stated how the shooting of Hanley by members of the Crown forces was "by way of a reprisal by the British for the shooting of an RIC sergeant named O'Donoghue by the IRA. earlier on the same night in the course of an IRA raid on Lunham's bacon factory".[137]

Hanley's mother Sarah Hanley filed a compensation claim for his death to the Free State Minister of Defence in 1923. The account as per her compensation claim stated: "The family was awakened by the breaking in of the bedroom door. A big man wearing the uniform of the RIC and goggles with a torch light in his hand stood in the centre of the room. The boy jumped out of bed shouting, 'Do not shoot me. I am an orphan and the chief support of my mother and sister'. At this point another man also in uniform entered the room. Two shots were fired, and the boy fell, wounded through the ear. When his mother lifted him from the floor the boy was dead".[138]

---

137 George Hurley, B.M.H. witness statement, July 15, 1957. (N.A.I., B.M.H, WS 1630), p. 4.

138 Hanley Sarah, Irish Military Archives, http://mspcsearch.militaryarchives.ie/docs/files//PDF_Pensions/R6/DP4150%20Patrick%20Hanley/2RBSD128%20Patrick%20Hanley.pdf, accessed July 12, 2022.

George Hurley informed John Watts in 1979 that Patrick Hanley was mentally slow, and despite an order at the time from the Cork city Fianna leadership that Na Fianna members should not wear their uniforms in public for fear of being marked out by Crown forces, that Hanley continued to be seen to wear his Fianna uniform around Cork city.

According to his mother's compensation application at the time of his death Patrick Hanley's earnings as a labourer in Cork city were one pound and fifteen shillings a week. Of this amount Patrick handed up one pound a week to his mother. His mother lost this income upon his death. In 1924, after submitting a claim to the Compensation (Personal Injuries) Committee, she received two hundred and fifty pounds (approximately eighteen thousand and five hundred euros in today's money). She had received nothing else before that so that amount served to cover her debts from the loss of one hundred and sixty pounds that she had lost out on from Patrick's wages since 1920 and left her with ninety pounds (six thousand and seven hundred euros). This was a once-off payment.

Ten years later in 1934, with the help of Former Cork city Fianna O/C Edward Gamble (who described her circumstances as "depressing"), she applied again to the Free State Department of Defence for a dependant's compensation. At this time, she was told to apply under the Army Pension Act. In December 1934, Mrs Hanley submitted a letter to the Department of Defence essentially begging for further compensation for her son's death. She stated "your aid may save me adding the poor house with its attendant horror of a pauper's burial to my few remaining days".

Four years passed with no change. In 1938, Mrs Hanley submitted another application under the 1937 Army Pensions Act. She received no response for two years and following requests from Mr. Gamble on her behalf, her application was considered and denied under Section 37 (3) (d) "that the yearly means of such person do not equal or exceed forty pounds". Mrs Hanley had an annual income of forty pounds and twelve shillings, hence in this instance she was twelve shillings over the limit. Her income was twenty-three pounds, nine shillings and three pence per year from the Old Age Pension, her earnings as a char woman was fifteen pounds, twelve shillings and ten pence, and the amount her unemployed (mentally disabled) adult daughter Ellen Hanley contributed was one pound and ten shillings.

In addition to her application in 1938, on 17 June 1940, Mrs Hanley submitted a letter to TD Thomas Dowdall (1870-1942) pleading her case and stating her health was fading.

On 18 June 1940, TD Dowdall sent a letter to Oscar Traynor, Minister for Defence. In the letter, Dowdall wrote to Minister Traynor that Patrick Hanley "shot a Sergeant O'Donoghue' and that "the young fellow was rather weak in the head, and was responsible for the deaths of O'Donoghue, Hanley, O'Connell and Colman by reason of his unauthorised act". [139]

On analysis of the evidence, this information stated by Dowdall to Traynor is inaccurate. There is no evidence or account of Patrick Hanley being present at the death of O'Donoghue on White Street on 17 November 1920. All witness statements and accounts confirm that this was an IRA shooting. Patrick Hanley was a Fianna boy, and only Operation Commanders (O/Cs) in Na Fianna had access to arms and ammunition. Hanley was not an O/C. Three Cork IRA men have since been determined to have been involved in the shooting of Sergeant O'Donoghue, and Patrick Hanley was not one of these three. Historian Peter Hart in his 1998 book 'The IRA & its Enemies', wrote that "Hanley was a target of the RIC by association".[140]

(Note - Mrs Susan (Sarah) Hanley never received an army dependant's pension from the Department of Defence. She died in Cork District Hospital on 25 December 1941. She is buried in an unmarked grave in the poor ground section of St Joseph's Cemetery in Cork city.)

---

139 Hanley Sarah, Irish Military Archives, http://mspcsearch.militaryarchives.ie/docs/files//PDF_Pensions/R6/DP4150%20Patrick%20Hanley/2RBSD128%20Patrick%20Hanley.pdf, accessed July 12, 2022.

140 Hart, Peter (1999), 'The I.R.A. & Its Enemies – Violence and Community in Cork 1916-1923', Clarendon Press, Oxford, p. 9.

George Hurley also stated that an additional reprisal raid occurred the same night as Hanley's shooting by the RIC in the Grattan Street area of Cork. This raid resulted in another Cork city Fianna boy named O'Brien being shot in the mouth. He however subsequently recovered from his wounds.

The notes of Denis Woods include reference to the Cork city Fianna representation at the funeral of Patrick Hanley: 20/11/1920 - Firing Party at P.Hanley Funeral (E.Gamble, D.McCarthy, D.Mulroy, D.Scully and D.Gamble).

Photo taken soon after the events of 18 November 1920.

Miss Ellen Hanley and Mrs Susan Hanley (sister and mother of Patrick Hanley) are second and third from the left.

Grave marker for Patrick Hanley

Republican plot, St Finbarr's Cemetery, Cork city

At the Republican Plot there are two memorials to Patrick's memory – an individual cross and a marble stone to Fianna Éireann. In addition, on 17 November 1957, a plaque was unveiled by Lord Mayor Jago in memory of Patrick Hanley on Patrick Hanley Buildings on Grattan Street.

CHAPTER TEN

In Summary

To conclude this study of the Cork city Fianna during the period 1910 to 1921, I will summarise some of the key findings from my research of the primary source material of military witness statements, pension and medal application records, witness interviews (conducted by John Watts in 1979) and the notes and correspondence of the Cork Fianna Éireann secretaries – Denis Woods and George Hurley:

1. The core function of the Cork city Fianna during the period 1919-1921 was to provide a supporting force for the two-city based IRA First Cork Brigade battalions. Between the Easter rising and the Truce on 11 July 1921, over five hundred people were killed in Cork by bullets or bombs, and an additional five hundred were wounded, Peter Hart wrote that "these numbers make the county by far the most violent place in Ireland in this period".[141] Cork city was no exception to this. The escalation and level of military operations within Cork city required an efficient and reliable military and intelligence support system for the IRA and the teenage boy scouts of the city's Fianna Éireann were tasked with this.

2. The total strength of the Fianna in Cork city at the time of the Truce has been estimated as approximately 100, however the core military support activities of the Fianna in Cork city during the most intense period of the conflict (1920-1921) were carried out by no more than 30 dedicated members. By the end of 1920, these members had formed an Active Service Unit of Na Fianna for the City. In his 1979 interview with John Watts, the former Cork

---

141 O'Conchubhair, Brian (Series Editor), 'Rebel Cork's Fighting Story 1916-1921' (2009), Mercier Press, p. 18.

Fianna John Murray recalled of the Cork Fianna ASU "they trained with small arms and rifles, and all had their own weapons which they stored in the graveyard of the Christian Brothers monastery. In time they became in effect a fulltime unit when forced to abandon their jobs and go on the run. Almost all Na Fianna's military assignments in 1921 were given to Active Service personnel, either independently or as members of IRA squads".

3. The link between the Cork city Fianna and the First and Second Battalions of the IRA First Cork Brigade was significantly closer than those of the IRA and Na Fianna in other areas and counties (with the possible exception of Dublin and Belfast). This existed partly due to the reportedly high transfer rate in Cork city of Na Fianna senior members to the IRA First Cork Brigade (over 50%) and also due to the close family and community connections between the members of the two organisations (often consisting of siblings, cousins, neighbours). The close proximity in age of the senior Fianna members in Cork city and the IRA members of the First and Second battalions was also undoubtedly a significant factor in the close relationship. Many of the IRA members were recent graduates of Na Fianna Éireann themselves, and so a level of respect and admiration existed between the two organisations that was noticeably absent elsewhere in the country.

4. Finally, it is the opinion of this author that an objective review of the extent of the military and support activities provided by the Active Service Unit of the Cork city Fianna during the years 1917 to 1921 could be described as 'Active Service' as per the criteria outlined by the Irish Department of Defence in 1955. Records exist of multiple instances of the Cork city Fianna participating in all of the qualifying activities as listed by the department, i.e. "attacking the enemy, obstructing communications, acquiring and transporting arms and ammunition, guarding prisoners, attending training camps and battalion or brigade meetings, carrying despatches, providing first aid, and assisting volunteers on the run".[142]

---

142 Coleman, Marie, 'Military Service Pension for Veterans of the Irish Revolution, 1916-1923', War in History, April 2013, Vol. 20, No. 2 (April 2013), p. 211, Sage Publications Ltd.

Bibliography

Archive Material:

- Activity Reports of First and 6th Battalions Cork First Brigade for July 1921, Mulcahy, P/7/A/23,

- Begley Correspondence in Department of Defence Series, A/07360,

- Irish Military Archives – Medal Series Collection – MD4942, (Denis Burke),

- Irish Military Archives – Medal Series Collection – MD41722, (Richard Keating),

- Irish Military Archives – Medal Series Collection – MD45105, (James Wickham),

- Irish Military Archives – Medal Series Collection – MD846, (Mark Wickham),

- Irish Military Archives – Medal Series Collection – MD23851, (Michael O'Donoghue),

- Irish Military Archives – Medal Series Collection – MD7157, (Jeremiah O'Shea),

- Irish Military Archives – Medal Series Collection – MD5203, (John Joseph O'Sullivan),

- Irish Military Archives – Military Service Pensions Collection – MA/ MSPC/FE/5,

- Irish Military Archives – Military Service Pensions Collection – MA/ MSPC/FE/8,

- Irish Military Archives – Military Service Pensions Collection – MA/MSPC/FE/40,

- Irish Military Archives – Military Service Pensions Collection – MA/MSPC/FE/41,

- Irish Military Archives – Military Service Pensions Collection– Reference number DP2685

- Seán Healy and Liam O'Callaghan, B.M.H. witness statement, October 04, 1947. (N.A.I., B.M.H, WS 47),

- Michael Lonergan, B.M.H. witness statement, August 01, 1948 (N.A.I., B.M.H., WS 140),

- Mark Wickham, B.M.H. witness statement, May 12, 1951 (N.A.I., B.M.H., WS 558),

- P.J. Murphy, B.M.H. witness statement, April 14, 1953. (N.A.1., B.M.H., WS 869),

- Patrick A. Murray, B.M.H. witness statement, February 26, 1957,

- James Allan Busby, B.M.H. witness statement, June 06, 1957. (N.A.I., B.M.H, WS 1628),

- Charles Meaney, B.M.H. witness statement, June 11, 1957. (N.A.I., B.M.H, WS 1631),

- Edward Horgan, B.M.H. witness statement, June 26, 1957. (N.A.I., B.M.H, WS 1644),

- George Hurley, B.M.H. witness statement, July 15, 1957. (N.A.I., B.M.H, WS 1630),

- Eamon Martin, B.M.H. witness statement, n.d. (N.A.I., B.M.H, WS 591)

Unpublished Material:
- Typed and handwritten notes, Denis Woods, Honourable Secretary, Na Fianna Éireann, Cork, 1934 – 1942.

Books Primary:

- Barry, Tom (1962), 'Guerilla Days in Ireland', Anvil Books Ltd

- O'Conchubhair, Brian (Series Editor), 'Rebel Cork's Fighting Story 1916-1921' (2009), Mercier Press

- The Central Council of Na Fianna Éireann (1914), 'Fianna Handbook'

Books Secondary:

- Bennett Richard (1995), 'The Black and Tans', Barnes and Noble, Inc.

- Cambell, Fergus (2005), 'Land and Revolution: Nationalist Politics in the West of Ireland, 1891–1921'

- Collins, M.E. (1993), 'History in The Making – Ireland 1868-1966', The Educational Company of Ireland

- Crowley, John, O'Drisceoil, Donal and Murphy, Mike (2017) 'Atlas of The Irish Revolution', New York University Press

- Hart, Peter (1999), 'The IRA & Its Enemies – Violence and Community in Cork 1916-1923', Clarendon Press, Oxford

- McCarthy, Kieran (2008), 'Republican Cobh and The East Cork Volunteers since 1913', Nonsuch Publishing

- Murphy, Gerard (2010), 'The Year of Disappearances – Political Killings in Cork 1921-1922', Gill and Macmillan

- O'Neill Tom (2006), 'The Battle of Clonmult – The IRA's Worst Defeat', Nonsuch Publishing Ltd.

- Sheehan, William (2011) 'A Hard Local War', The History Press Ireland

- Tierney, Mark (1987), 'Ireland since 1870', C J Fallon

- Townshend, Charles (1975), 'The British Campaign in Ireland, 1919-1921, The Development of Political and Military Policies, Oxford University Press

Journals and Articles:

- Bustolin, Vitelio, 'Criteria for defining War, Terrorism, and Guerilla Warfare based on Clausewitz's concepts on the nature and essence of War', R. Esc. Guerra Nav., Rio de Janeiro, v. 25, n.3, pp. 643-673, 2019

- Coleman, Marie, 'Military Service Pension for Veterans of the Irish Revolution, 1916-1923', War in History, April 2013, Vol. 20, No. 2 (April 2013), pp. 201-221, Sage Publications Ltd.

- Cremin, Maura R, 'Fighting on Their Own Terms: The Tactics of the Irish Republican Army 1919 – 1921', Small Wars and Insurgencies, 26:6, pp. 912-936, (2015)

- Hay, Marnie, 'The foundation and development of Na Fianna Éireann, 1909-16', Irish Historical Studies, xxxvi, no. 141 (May 2008)

- Kalyanaraman, S, 'Conceptualisations of Guerrilla Warfare', Strategic Analysis, Vol.27, No.2, Apr - Jun 2003, The Institute for Defence Studies and Analyses

- Morrison, Eve (2016) 'Chapter Eight - Witnessing the Republic: the Ernie O'Malley Notebook Interviews and the Bureau of Military History Compared', pp. 124-140, In 'Cormac K.H. O'Malley and John P. Waters (eds.), Modern Ireland and Revolution: Ernie O'Malley in Context', Dublin: Irish Academic Press.

- Townshend, Charles, 'The Irish Republican Army and the Development of Guerrilla Warfare, 1916-1921', The English Historical Review, Vol. 94, Third71, Apr 1979, pp. 318 – 345, Oxford University Press.

PhD Thesis:

- Watts, John R. (1981) 'Na Fianna Éireann: A Case Study of a Political Youth Organisation', University of Glasgow

On-line Material:

- 'Christmas Eve, 1920: Armed men attack Examiner offices', https://www.irishexaminer.com/news/spotlight/arid-40196055.html

- 'Make way for the Molly Maguires!' The Ancient Order of Hibernians and the Irish Parliamentary Party, 1902–14' https://www.historyireland.com/make-way-for-the-molly-maguires-the-ancient-order-of-hibernians-and-the-irish-parliamentary-party-1902-14/,

- Remembering 1920: The inquest jury speaks', https://www.corkindependent.com/2020/04/23/remembering-1920-the-inquest-jury-speaks/

- 'Rowdy rebels - the formation of the Irish Volunteers in Cork city', https://www.irishcentral.com/roots/history/rowdy-rebels-formation-irish-volunteers-cork-city

- THE HISTORY OF NA FIANNA ÉIREANN IN CORK CITY 1910-1924' https://FiannaÉireannhistory.wordpress.com/2016/10/06/the-history-of-na-Fianna-Éireann-in-cork-city-1910-1924/

- 'The Irish Revolution Project' https://www.ucc.ie/en/theirishrevolution/collections/cork-fatality-register/register-index/1921-188/,

- The Irish War', https://www.theirishwar.com/product/comrac-bar-for-the-black-tan-medal-comrac-bar-19171921/.

- Hanley Sarah, Irish Military Archives, http://mspcsearch.militaryarchives.ie/docs/files//PDF_Pensions/R6/DP4150%20Patrick%20Hanley/2RBSD128%20Patrick%20Hanley.pdf

- Creedon, Conal '1916 Rising Cork', Youtube, uploaded by Irishtown Productions, January 08, 2020, https://www.youtube.com/watch?v=X59c4egVjJI.

Please Review

Dear reader,

Thank you for taking the time to read this book. I would really appreciate if you could spread the word about it and if you purchased it online, if you would leave a review.

Colmán de Róiste

Appendix 1

Republican Activities and Related Fianna Involvement in Cork city

(01/04/1916 –11/07/1921)

(Extracted from Denis Woods' typed notes, composed 1934 to 1943)

01/04/1916 - 30/04/1917	• General training, propaganda work, public parading • Date unnamed – Removing arms from Sheares Street to 145 Evergreen Road – J.O'Brien (21 Douglas Street), P.Vaughan (Douglas Street), Seán Healy (Barrack Street), T O'Sullivan (Deceased), • Date Unnamed – Storing and Carrying arms for Fianna – J.O'Brien (21 Douglas Street) • Special Duty at Sheares Street – E.Murray
23/04/1916	Ordered to proceed to Macroom with Irish Volunteers – M.J.O'Sullivan, J.Callaghan, A.Busby, L. Hennessy, S.Healy, L.O'Callaghan and others unnamed
08/05/1916	Searches for arms by British military and police in city. Volunteers. Wickham, Sheridan, Tom and Michael Harris and Chris Hamilton arrested.
11/05/1916	Tómas Mac Curtain arrested in Cork city
18/05/1916	Asquith in Cork. Conference with Lord Mayor Butterfield and Bishop
30/05/1916	Conference in Volunteer Hall, Lord Mayor and Bishop proposed surrender of all arms to be held by them
01/06/1916	Lord Mayor informed Military authorities that Volunteers refused to surrender arms
05/06/1916	Some prisoners from City and County gaols released
14/07/1916	Release of southern prisoners and their arrival in Cork. Attempted meeting in Grand Parade dispersed by the police. Recruiting office attacked and damaged.
25/07/1916	Release of Cork prisoners from Frongoch
08/10/1916	J. (Seán) Hegarty arrested in Ballingeary
24/11/1916	Drilling Prohibited
29/12/1916	Military equipment taken from soldiers by civilians
03/01/1917	P. Corcoran printer, arrested. Plant removed to Barracks
23/02/1917	Terence McSweeney, Tomás Mac Curtain, Seán Nolan and P.Hourihan arrested and removed to military barracks
26/03/1917	Patrick Higgins, Dominick Street, Jas Courtney, John Healy arrested
01/04/1917 - 31/03/1918	Removing and carrying arms from Evergreen Road to Industry Street – J O'Brien (21 Douglas Street) and Seán Healy (Barrack Street)

04/1917 – 03/1918	• Activities – General obstruction of recruiting meetings, hold up and taking equipment off RIC. and soldiers, General Training and Parades • (Easter 1917) Uniformed Parading in face of Proclamation for the anniversary of Easter Rising • (22 Nov 1917) Uniformed Parading on 50-year anniversary of Manchester Martyrs
04/06/1917	Volunteer Hall closed. J Donovan, C Murphy, Jas Walsh, D. O'Callaghan and William Power arrested
25/06/1917	Bayonet charge in Cork
03/07/1917	Hunger Strike Cork Gaol
12/07/1917	Volunteer parade in Cork re Clare Election Victory
05/09/1917	Police enquiries re raid on Grammar school
24/09/1917	Sgt Desmond, Victoria Cross attacked and wounded
27/09/1917	Parade re death of Tom Ashe. Rosary recited at National Monument by Tomás Mac Curtain.
29/09/1917	Baton charge at Clarkes Bridge under D.I. Swansey
16/10/1917	Cork prisoners on hunger strike
22/10/1917	Parade of Volunteers from Sheares Street, Hall.
02/11/1917	Arrest of J.Murphy and Bob Langford
27/11/1917	Blackrock castle commandeered by military
10/12/1917	Address of meeting by DeValera in Cork
1918 - 1919	Dates Unnamed - Church Door Collections for Fianna Funds - Several arrested
06/01/1918	Soldiers attacked in streets, Baton charge by RIC.
04/1918 – 03/1919	• General election work, anniversary parades in the face of enemy proclamation, propaganda, training in the use of arms, effacing enemy poster (proclamations). Obstructing RIC. and Military • Date unnamed – Taking equipment off military – E. Gamble, C. Meaney, C.Curtain, S.Wall and L.Cahill
14/04/1918	Anti-Conscription meeting called for National Monument
06/09/1918	Terence McSweeney arrested and deported to England
12/09/1918	Soldier disarmed at Richmond Hill, Cork of his rifle.
26/10/1918	Richard Moynihan, Old Youghal Rd, Cork charged for possession of a revolver.
05/11/1918	Hd. Const Clarke shot in Leitrim Street, McNeilus arrested
11/11/1918	McNeilus escapes from Cork Gaol. Sgt Burke, Ballincollig injured when trying to disarm firing part at funeral.
17/11/1918	Volunteer Perry, Bachelors Quay buried with full military honours
1919 - 1921	Intelligence Operations (IO Work): • Keeping tans under observation in public house on South Main Street (D.Scully, J.Carey, C O'Brien, D.Gamble, M. O'Leary)

	• IO Work on HERD (E.Warren) • IO Work on Begley (S.Walsh, D.Scully, D.Gamble, R.Flynn, M Leary, E.Gamble) • IO Work on Madden (W Rose, T.Donovan, R.Mahoney) • IO Work on Murphy (T Donovan, W Rose, R.Mahoney) • IO Work on Linehan (T.Barrett, D.Scully, M Leary, E.Gamble, S.Wall and P. Lynch) • IO Work on Farrell and Podesta (D. Scully, S.Wall, P.Lynch, L.Cahill, E.Gamble, D.Woods and D.Gamble • IO Work on Hoare (T.Barrett) • IO Work on McGiff (D. Scully, W.Quirke, E.Murray, D.Gamble) • IO Work on Sullivan (T.Donovan and W.Rose) • IO Work on Poland (E.Gamble, L.Cahill, D.Scully, D.Gamble, T.Twomey) • IO Work on Good (E.Murray, E.Gamble, J.Peirce, J,Carey, D.Scully, D.Gamble and M/O'Leary) • IO Work on D.Donovan (Shot) (E.Gamble, D.Gamble, M O'Leary, S.Wall, D.Scully, T.Cahill and C.Curtain) • IO Work on Sherlock (Shot) (E Gamble) • IO Work on Casey (Gratton Street) (E.Gamble, C.O'Brien, D.Woods, D.Gamble, J.Peirce)
04/1919 to 03/1920	• Raid on Tract shop – a number of important and useful books were seized including military training books (Armed E.Gamble, D.Scully and E.Murray, unarmed – L.Cahill, D.Mulroy, S.Wall) • Holding up soldiers and taking equipment off them (C.Curtain, C.Meaney and S.Wall) • Removal of explosives from Andy Aherns on Grattan Street to Rathmore Terrace, (L.Clay, J.Peirce, E.Keating, M.O'Leary, E.Gamble, D.Gamble, D.Scully, E.Denny, C.O'Brien and S.Walsh) • Scouting and mobilising for IRA (J.Foley) • Armed raid on the Baden Powell rooms South Mall seized dummy rifles, bayonets and equipment (raided several times) (P.Lynch, E.Gamble, C.Curtain, W.Quirke, D.Gamble, C.Woods, S.Walsh, D.Scully, E.Murray, J.Pierce, M.O'Leary, C.Herlihy)
14/05/1919	Patients in hospital after Gratton St explosion improving
16/05/1919	Fred Murray charged with shooting policeman
17/05/1919	Patient in Gratton street explosion removed from North Infirmary
19/05/1919	Tom Ashe club and Sinn Féin club raided by police
20/07/1919	Soldiers attacked. Const Keogh received bullet in thigh. Military officer attacked in Victoria Hotel
04/11/1919	Arms and Ammunition captured off boat in Passage docks.
18/11/1919	Gillabbey cross blown up. Murray gun shop raided.
23/11/1919	Manchester Martyrs demonstration proclaimed by military

05/01/1920	Inchigeela Barracks attacked and captured. Arms (etc) removed
13/01/1920	Ed.Horgan escapes from Mercy Hospital. On trial for raid of arms
31/01/1920	Tómas Mac Curtain was unanimously elected Lord Mayor of Cork
17/02/1920	Policeman held up and post bag taken with mail for Union Quay
18/02/1920	Sinn Féin Club raided by police. Four men arrested.
25/02/1920	Quilisk shooting
11/03/1920	D.I. McDonagh shot – seriously wounded, Sgt. Ferris escaped
20/03/1920	Const. Murtagh shot dead at Popes quay
30/03/1920	Dwyer, Pouladuff shot dead at home
31/03/1920	Terry McSweeney elected Lord Mayor in place of Tomás Mac Curtain who was murdered on March 20, 1920.
April 1920 – March 1921	• Assisting Irish Republican Courts collecting fines and prisoners (General for Fianna A.S.U.) • Raid on the railway for Boycott Newspapers and commandeering the van, papers dumped in the river (Armed – S.Wall, S.Walsh, P.Lynch, D.Woods; Unarmed – D.Milroy, R.Cremin and J.Murray) • Guarding prisoner (a civilian) at Blackrock Castle overnight (D.Woods and S.Wall) • Guarding prisoner at McGurks, North Main Street (P.Lynch, E.Gamble, D.Gamble, D.Scully and others) • Seizing of cycles from known Loyalists throughout the city (continuous for Fianna A.S.U – First and Second Battalions) • Seizing of motor cycles from W.F.O'Connor (E.Gamble and J.Kickham – G Company, First Battalion, Cork First IRA Brigade) • Raids on Lesters chemist for boycott goods (P.Lynch, S.Walsh and R.Flynn – all armed) • Raids on the city shops for Gallaghers cigarettes and boycott goods on several occasions (Armed – E.Gamble, P.Lynch, D.Woods, S.Walsh, D.Scully, S.Wall; Unarmed – L.Cahill and R.Flynn) • Raid on Blair's Chemist for Boycott Goods (Armed – S.Walsh, S.Wall, D.Woods, E.Gamble, R.Flynn) • Raid on Maynes Chemist for Boycott goods (Armed – S.Wall, R.Flynn, J.Murray and S.Walsh) • Raid on Fieldings Patrick Street for Boycott Goods (raided at least twice) (Armed – S.Wall, S.Walsh, D.Scully, D.Woods, P.Lynch, E.Gamble, R.Flynn; Unarmed – G.Hurley and C.Curtain) • Raid on Burkes Chemist for Boycott Goods (Armed – P.Lynch, S.Walsh, D.Woods, D.Scully, S.Wall and E.Gamble; G.Hurley, C.Curtain and J.Sheehan) • Removing arms from Grave to Hibernian Buildings (E.Murray – Washington Street) • Removing arms from Maylor Street to Parliament Street (around time /night of burning of cork – December 11, 1920) (D.Woods and D.Scully)

- Supplying IRA with scrap metal and materials (J.Mullins, E.Warren, E.Gamble, S.Walsh and R.Flynn)
- Raid on Shines College Road – Result 1 Shot Gun (Armed – F.Nolan, W.Ross, T.Donovan, C. Meaney, J.Fennell, R.Mahoney, W.Quirke, J.Cummans)
- Raid on Rifle Range – Glen, Cork Barracks, Result 90 Rounds Ammunition (Armed – S.Walsh and 2 others unnamed) (note – no ammunition recovered there)
- Blocking Roads (W.Dennehy, W.Hurley)
- Housing WJ Barry – Foreman of Jury on Inquest of Thomas McCurtain – 42 Maylor Street (D.Scully and D.Woods)
- Raid for arms holding up ex-soldiers at St Mary's Hall and taking revolvers off them (S.Walsh and P.Lynch)
- Raid for arms taking revolver off suspect (Sullivan) at Pine Street (Armed – S.Walsh, J.Carey, E.Gamble, P.lynch, non-armed – D.Gamble and R.Flynn)
- Removing ammunition from Drinan street to Lee Road for IRA (W.Dennehy)
- Removing 3 revolvers and ammunition from Hillgrove Lane to Blackpool N.S. (E.Heagerty, S.Wall, M.O'Leary)
- Removing arms from Fair Hill to CAFÉ NA CUIN and back again for IRA A.S.U. (Jim O'Leary Hall and Washington Street) (T.Barrett)
- Carried bombs to Washington street for G.Company Ambush Party (C.Curtain and E.Gamble)
- Holding arms for IRA (W.Dennehy, S.Wall, J.Foley, E.Gamble, D.Woods, D.Scully, T.Donovan)
- Raids for Boycott newspapers waylaid vans at St Patricks Church and dumped them in the river (Armed – E.Gamble, D.Scully, D.Woods, R.Flynn, S.Wall, S.Walsh)
- Removing shot gun and ammunition from Adelaide Street to Grand Parade for IRA G.Company
- Removing of Company dump from Gamblers on Gratton Street to Coach Street (E.Gamble in charge, several members of Fianna engaged)
- Continuous raids on food supplies intended for RIC Barracks the raids were carried out on the shops or on the vans:
  - Names of the Shops – Hogans on Castle Street, O'Sullivan on Paul Street, Baltimore Stores on McCurtain Street, Barry on Douglas Street, Lunhams on White Street, O'Sullivan's on Oliver Plunkett Street, Buckley on Oliver Plunkett Street, Collins on Castle Street. (On Raids – T.Barrett, J.Murray, T.Murray, J.O'Sullivan, E.Hegarty)
- Raids on Dobbins Alfred Street for Boycott goods (Armed – C.Curtain, S.Walsh, T.Forde, P.Lynch, J.Foley, D.Milroy)
- Continuous – Holding up loyalists for their cycles (Armed – F.Nolan, W.Rose, C.Meaney, T.Donovan, unarmed – R.Mahoney, J.Fennell)
- Removing arms from T.O'Sullivan's (Brigade O.C. Fianna) - Douglas Street to Hibernian Buildings (E.Murray)

	• Arresting and Conveying suspects believed to have arms to Cork Park and interrogating them (Armed – S.Walsh, D.Woods, R.Flynn, P.Lynch and S.Wall) • Armed attack on soldiers, result – wounding one on Wellington Road, (Armed – C.Meaney, C.Curtain, F.Nolan, W.Rose) • Dislocating telephone wires (W.Dennehy, T.Donovan, W.Rose, C.Meaney) • Scouting for IRA Ambush parties (T.Barrett, E.Gamble, L.Cahill) – (Note – T.Barrett once under fire from armoured company while acting as a scout for an O'Connell Street ambush) • Raid on pension office - South Mall seized typewriters, writing material, list of names of British ex-servicemen (Armed: D.Scully, F.McMahon, S.Wall. S.Walsh, E.Gamble, Unarmed – E.Murray, L.Clay, D.Gamble, W.Quirke, J.Peirce, P.Lynch) • Burning Mail baskets and 2 trucks (Baskets at GPO, Trucks at Phoenix Street) • (Armed – C.Meaney, F.Nolan, E.Murray, Unarmed – W.Rose, C.Curtain, W.Martin, T.Donovan, W.Quirke) • Disarming Black and Tan at Court House (obtained a revolver) (Armed – S.Walsh, Unarmed – J.Carey, M.O'Leary) • Disarming Black and Tan at Kyrls Quay (revolver) (Armed – E.Gamble, S.Walsh, unarmed – D.Gamble, P.Lynch, G.Hurley, E.Keating, L.Clay, S.Walsh) • Disarming Black and Tan at Maylor Street (revolver) (Armed – S.Walsh, unarmed – E.Gamble, J.Carey, P.Lynch, E.Keating) • Assisting in burning of Income Tax office (Armed – F.McMahon, unarmed – E.Gamble) • Removal of ammunition and explosives from SS Elblana to Drinan Street (E.Gamble, J.O'Brien, P. Grant (B company IRA)) • Removing arms and ammunition from F.Murray's house to North Main Street on 2 occasions (J.Murray)
05/04/1920	Income Tax offices and South Mall and South Terrace burned. Togher RIC Barracks burned
09/04/1920	Correspondence captured ordering arrest of all Sinn Féiners
24/04/1920	Solider fired at and wounded near Cork Barracks
12/05/1920	Sgt Garvey and Const Harrington shot dead. Doyle wounded
14/05/1920	Commons RIC Barracks burned down, also Dublin Pike.
03/06/1920	Blarney Barracks attacked.
24/06/1920	Blackrock RIC Barracks burned down
25/06/1920	Military car taken at Glanmire station
01/07/1920	King Street Barracks.
05/07/1920	Soldiers' cycles taken at Western Road
12/07/1920	King Street, St Luke's Lower Road, Barracks burned
14/07/1920	Blackrock Road Barracks burned
15/07/1920	Two military lorries captured and burned at Dennehy's cross

19/07/1920	Smith shot at CO Club; CO Inspector Craig wounded
02/08/1920	Whites Cross Ambush
04/08/1920	Curfew patrol fired at in Blackpool
05/08/1920	Curfew patrol fired at in Blackpool, fire returned
07/08/1920	Curfew patrol fired on at Bachelors Quay
09/08/1920	Curfew patrol fired on at Cattle Lane
10/08/1920	Curfew patrol fired on at Coliseum
23/08/1920	DI Swansey shot at Lisburn
30/08/1920	Curfew patrol fired at in Blackpool
03/09/1920	Petrol taken from IA Oil Company. Military guard at Gaol wounded
13/09/1920	Several houses raided in Douglas for arms
24/09/1920	Mails taken from Military Sergeant in Winthrop Street
25/09/1920	Attack on General Strickland
06/10/1920	Military attacked at Viaduct
09/10/1920	Barrack ambush
19/10/1920	Mails raided at Cork station; Military goods also taken
25/10/1920	Terence McSweeney dies on Hunger Strike in Brixton jail
11/11/1920	Military stores taken from C and K Rly
16/11/1920	Two men kidnapped from train at Ballinhassig
17/11/1920	Four staff officers kidnapped at Waterfall
18/11/1920	Sgt O'Donoghue shot dead at White Street
20/11/1920	Firing Party at P.Hanley Funeral (E.Gamble, D.McCarthy, D.Milroy, D.Scully and D.Gamble)
22/11/1920	Constable Ryan kidnapped at Lower Rd Cork
25/11/1920	Donoghue, Trahy and Hehigan killed by Bomb
26/11/1920	Co. Inspector shot on South Mall
27/11/1920	Two killed at Dan O'Leary's at Blackpool by bomb
30/11/1920	Tom Ashe club burned
01/12/1920	North Abbey Barracks attacked. Blemings Killed, Fleming shot in Water Street
09/12/1920	G. Horgan kidnapped
13/12/1920	Dillons Cross ambush
28/12/1920	Examiner office plant wrecked
05/01/1921	Parnell bridge ambush
10/01/1921	Constable Carroll and attendant Sheehan wounded
17/01/1921	Mailiff and Ryan shot in Washington Street
30/01/1921	C.B. Rly raided and Military stores taken
10/02/1921	Riley, Douglas shot dead

14/02/1921	O'Leary clerk at Military barracks shot at and seriously wounded
15/02/1921	William O'Sullivan found shot at Tory Top Lane
16/02/1921	Chas Beale found shot at Wilton. Attack on Military at Vernon Mount Lodge. Lodge blown up
18/02/1921	Mrs Lindsay and Chauffeur kidnapped
19/02/1921	M. Walsh taken from Cork union and shot
21/02/1921	Mulhally taken from South Infirmary and shot dead.
22/02/1921	Body of Finbarr O'Sullivan found near Douglas
23/02/1921	D. McDonald wounded. Capture of men at Mrs McKay's at Cork
26/02/1921	Ambush at Ballyvourney
01/03/1921	Reprisals for Dripsey executions
02/03/1921	Charlie Daly shot at Cork station
05/03/1921	Curfew patrol attacked at Shandon Street
11/03/1921	John Good, Labour Exchange shot at Tower Street
15/03/1921	Charles Murray shot dead near Victoria Barracks
21/03/1921	Con Sheehan Mental Hospital shot dead
23/03/1921	Raids Glanmire and Bandon railway stations
23/03/1921	Six men shot at Ballycannon
25/03/1921	Attempt to rescue prisoners at Cork Gaol. Poland's body found by police.
30/03/1921	Raid at Killens

04/1921 – 07/1921	• Raid on the Grammar School - 2 Bicycles seized – J.Foley and D.O'Mahoney.
	• Under Arms to Shoot Blennerhasset – E.Gamble, C.Hurley and IRA Members (unnamed)
	• Date Unnamed - Holding up laundry van on Brian Boru Bridge on the way to RIC. Barracks – J.Foley (armed) and D.O'Mahoney
	• Several occasions – Holding up lines men taking apparatus off them Watercourse Road and Commons road – D.Mulroy (armed), J.Foley, S.Wall (armed)
	• Hand-painting posters at own house and posting up around city – T.Donovan, W.Rose, J.Fennell, R.Mahoney and M.Riordan
	• Dates Unnamed
	  • Armed duty at Grand Parade – T.O'Donovan (armed), J.Fennell, M.Riordan, W.Rose (armed) and R.Mahoney (armed)
	  • Reprisals for Dripsey Ambush scouting – S.Walsh and E.Gamble (both armed)
	  • Raids on Sheehan South Main Street for Boycott Goods (Jam) – listed as raided several times – S.Walsh (armed), E.Gamble (armed), D.Scully (armed), J.Foley, L.Cahill, T.Forde, D.Gamble, D.Milroy, D.Woods (armed), R.Flynn, P.Lynch (armed), S.Wall, J.Murray, C.Curtain (armed) and RM Cremin

04/1921 – 07/1921	• Under orders awaiting arrest of suspects Farrell and Podesta at Blackpool during curfew – D.Woods (armed), J.Foley (armed), D.O'Mahoney, S.Wall (armed) and R.Flynn (armed) • Sent to Tivoli with instructions to waylay Farrell and Podesta and shoot them – S.Walsh, P.Lynch, T.Forde (all armed) • Dislocating telephone service – (continuous) – D.Milroy (armed), T.Donovan (armed), J.Murray, W.Dennehy, L.Cahill (armed), S.Wall (armed), E.Gamble (armed) and W.Rose (armed) • Housing armed party of IRA (B Company) at 42 Maylor street – D. Woods and D.Scully – All members of Active Service Unit held arms • Armed attack on Tan wounding him at South Main Street (E.Gamble and C.O'Brien) • Burning Military car outside courthouse (E.Gamble, J.O'Sullivan, E.Keating and C.O'Brien – (Burned by Jo Mahony and Keating – G Company) • Armed Raid on Burns East View Terrace (W.Rose (armed), J.Fennel (armed), T.Donovan (armed), R.Mahoney) • Raid on the Railway for boycott goods (threads) (Armed – P.Lynch and S.Walsh) • Raid on News Bros for Boycott Newspapers and dumped same in the river
05/04/1921	Jas Flynn wounded at Blarney Road
09/04/1921	House of C.J. Young, Carrigbawn, Blackrock Rd, burned
13/04/1921	Const Plaice wounded near Co. Gaol; Two police lorries bombed at Washington street
14/04/1921	Body of DS Donovan, Barrack Street found near Ballygarvan
15/04/1921	Lorry of Bacon for military burned
18/04/1921	Const McDonald was fired at in Cove Street
20/04/1921	Tadg Sullivan shot in Douglas Street
25/04/1921	Mailbags taken throughout the city
28/04/1921	Military stores taken at C and B Rly
03/05/1921	Mails taken at Blackrock Road and Douglas
05/05/1921	Night mail held up at Rathpeacon, 6 cases of military stores taken (searchlight apparatus)
09/05/1921	Sterland shot at Cook Street. John Purcell found shot, Tory Top Lane
12/05/1921	Bicycles taken at Blackrock and Douglas
16/05/1921	Fr. O'Callaghan shot dead. O'Connell street, Ambush (Fianna had no connection with ambush, involved that night in making a dug out for dumping arms – L.Cahill, D.Milroy, J.Foley, S.Wall and E.Hegarty (all armed).
17/05/1921 - 22/05/1921	Two men Hawkins shot
18/05/1921 - 22/05/1921	Two bombs thrown at Military officer's car in Washington Street. Patrick Keating shot at Shandon Street. Attempt to burn mails in GPO Cork

23/05/1921	Carload English papers taken at Bowling Green Street and destroyed
24/05/1921	Stephen Dorman wounded Douglas Street, died
25/05/1921	Dinneen's, Shandon Street, Mannixs, Sheehans and Caseys burned
27/05/1921	Dobbins, Pikes, Simpsons, and Jakobs and Douglas Golf Pavilion burned
28/05/1921	O'Sullivan Blarney Street found shot Model farm road.
31/05/1921	Mails taken from Muskerry tram at Victoria Cross
08/06/1921	Moores hotel and Hibernian Hall occupied by Crown Forces
09/06/1921	Two constables attacked in Bandon Road
10/06/1921	Thomas O'Keeffe, Corporation Buildings shot dead at Ballyvolane. Healy, Watercourse Road, wounded and removed to hospital
13/06/1921	Stensons Douglas Street raided, two wounded
22/06/1921	Four Licensed premises and two cycle shops closed by Military
24/06/1921	General attacks on RIC Barracks, Cork
29/06/1921	Leo Murphy shot dead at Waterfall
08/07/1921	Spriggs shot at Blarney Street.
09/07/1921	Irish Bulletin states a Truce is being arranged
11/07/1921	Capture of Spy (Begley) - E.Gamble (armed), R.Flynn, S.Walsh (armed), D.Scully (armed), L.Clay and D.Gamble
11/07/1921	Details of Truce published

Appendix 2 (Typed)

Old Fianna Unit, 12 Morrison's Island, Cork

Old IRA Men's Association
(Cork No.1 Brigade)

09 July, 1942

Re: Fianna Applicants in receipt of Statutory 21 days notice, list of whom are attached

A Chara,

The total strength of the Fianna in Cork city on the 11th July, 1921 was 1100 and in view of this fact alone we cannot understand the reason why your board has not recognised the Fianna in Cork as one of the military organisations that were responsible for that measure of freedom this country gained as a result of the combined actions of these organisations. Up to date only two officers of the Fianna in Cork have been given an award and the remaining applicants (approx. 14) are in receipt of statutory 21 day notices.

The activities of Fianna in Cork were subject to the Brigade Council IRA, and they were strictly confined to a series of activities which they (the brigade) laid down for them, as it was considered that it was in their sphere, they would usefully serve the cause. These outlined activities were Intelligence such as observation of spies and suspected spies, observation of enemy posts and patrols, sorting and carrying orders for IRA ambush parties, storing arms, raids on enemy food supplies, raid for arms (etc) (etc) (see reference enclosed). As a result of their activities several Fianna were arrested and imprisoned.

It is very unfair that your board have placed (as apparently, they have done) the Fianna applications on as high a level as those of the IRA. The injustice of this is brought home when the age of the applicants is considered, few if any of them having reached their twenties on the 11th July 1921. We would therefore urge your board when considering the appeal of these applicants to give the stated grounds your considerable attention.

D.Woods
Honourable Secretary, Cork Fianna Éireann

To: M.Cummins
Office of Dept Defence
Military Service Pension Board

Appendix 2 (Original Part 1)

Cumann na Sean Óglac

Old I.R.A. Men's Association

(CORK No. 1 BRIGADE)

Old Fianna Unit

Wallace Chambers
~~12 MORRISON'S ISLAND,~~
Marlboro St. Cork

Cork, 9th July 1942

Re Fianna applicants in receipt of Statutory 21 Days notice, list of whom are attached.

A chara,

The total strength of the Fianna in Cork city on the 11th July 1921 was 1,100 and in view of this fact alone we cannot understand the reason why your board has not recognised the Fianna in Cork as one of the military organisations that were responsible for that measure of freedom this country gained as a result of the combined activities of these organisations.

Up to date only two officers of the Fianna in Cork have been given an award and the remaining applicants (approx 14) are in receipt of Statutory 21 Day notice.

The activities of Fianna in Cork were subject to the Brigade Council I.R.A. and they were strictly confined to a series of activities which the I.R.A. (the Brigade) laid down for them, as it was considered that it was in these spheres they would most usefully serve the cause. These outlined activities were Intelligence such as Observation of spies & suspected spies, Observation of enemy posts & patrols, scouting & carrying arms for I.R.A. ambush parties, storing arms, raids for Boycott goods, raids on Enemy food supplies, raids for arms etc etc. (see reference enclosed).

As a result of these activities several

Appendix 2 (Original Part 2)

Fianna were arrested and imprisoned.

"It is very unfair that your board have placed (as apparently they have done) the Fianna applications on as high a level as those of the I.R.A. The injustice of this is brought home when the age of the applicants is considered, few if any of them having reached their twenties on the 11th July 1921

we would therefore urge your board when considering the appeals of these applicants to give the foregoing points your considerate attention

[signature]

D. Woods.   Hon Sec.

To. M. Cremin
Office of the Referee
Military Service Pension Board

Appendix 3

2. 11/7/1921

1s. 1921.

rigade Comdt.-- P. Kennahon/E. Gamble.
" Adjt D. Scully.   Organiser--J. Carey.
" I.O. M. O'Leary   A. S. U. O/C. S. WALSH.
" Q.M. F. Lynch (acting)

1st. Battalion.

Comdt   Comdt.   E. Gamble / D. Mulroy.
           Vice   D. Mulroy.
           Adjt   L. Cahill. (Died)
           I. O.   C. Curtain.
           Q. M.   F. Lynch. 105 Commons Rd Cork E/0246

A. COMPANY.	B. COMPANY.	C. COMPANY.
Capt S. Walsh.	Capt. D. Woods	Capt. J. Murray/C. O'Leary
1st. Lt. E. Kelleher	Lieut R. Flynn	Lieut T. O'Callaghan.
2nd. Lt V. O'Leary.	Adjt J. Wickham.	Adjt D. O'Callaghan.
Adjt J. Pyne.	Q. M. J. Caulfield.	Q. M. L W. Danahy.
Q. M. R. Busteed.	1. O'S T. Carroll	1. O8s L. Cahill.
1. O's F. Slattery	C. Kenneally.	T. Keohane.
J. Phibbs.		

D. COMPANY.	E? COMPANY No. 1.	E. COMPANY NO. 2.
Capt Bap Lynch.	Capt V. Stack	Capt T. Forde/J. Foley
Lieut P. J. Cronin.	Lieut M. O'Neill,	Lieut J. Foley.
Adjt T. McCarthy.	Q. M. Do.	2nd. C. McCarthy
1. O8s V. Foley.	Adjt T. Burns.	Adjt . Ryan.
T. Barrett.		Q. M. C. Quialann.
		1. O's J. Sullivan
		R. Cronin.

G. COMPANY.	H. COMPANY.
Capt D. Gamble (Surrendered)	Capt P. Young/N. Horgan.
Lt. J. Pierce. (Died)	Lt. E. Uniacke
Adjt R. Lee.	2nd J. Cross
Q. M. L. Clay.	Q. M. E. Callinan.
I. O. R. Hurley.	Adjt E. Warren.

----------------o----------------

FIRST BATTALION COMPRISED 8 COMPANIES AND STRENGTH IS AS FOLLOWS.

A COMPANY	120.
B COMPANY	45
C COMPANY	50
D. COMPANY	110
E. COY. 1 & 2	130
G. COMPANY	80
H. COMPANY	80
TOTAL STRENGTH OF BN.	615.

Appendix 4

Cork Brigade Fianna Eireann.

Ist. Batt Area.

1917/18.

Sean Mac Dirmuid Sluagh.
Capt. Frank Mac Mahon.
Ist. Lieut Sean Scully.
2nd. " C. Woods.

1919.

Capt Sean Scully.
Ist. Lieut C Woods.
2nd. " Michael Delea.

1917/21.

Clegheen Sluagh.
Capt. Sean Mullins. Barretts Buildings Blarney St. Cork.
Ist. Lieut. John Carroll.
2nd. " A. Corcoran. U.S.A.

1919/20.

Capt. Ed. Gamble.
Ist. Lieut Dan Scully.
2nd. " D. Woods.

1921.

Capt. Dan Scully.
Ist. Lieut D. Woods.
2nd. 2 Dan Gamble.

Brigade Staff 1917/18.

Comdt Of Munster, Seumas Courtney. Deceased.
Cork Brigade Area. Comdt. Tagh O. Sullivan.
Killed By Black & Tans. At
Douglas St. Cork. 1921.
Adjt. Richard Murphy. Deceased.
Q/Master. Patrick Murray.

On the 5/9/21, Edward Gamble Was Suspended from all
Services in Fianna.

2nd. Batt Area.

1917/18.

Con. Colbert Sluagh.
Capt. Dan Mac Sweeney. Australia.
Ist. Lieut. M. Donovan. Murphys Cottages Evergreen Cork,
2Nd. " Ed. Murray. 5. Washington St. Cork.

1919.

Capt. Dan Mac Sweeney.
Ist. Lieut. Ed. Murray.
2nd, " Tom. Twomey.

1920.

Capt. Ed. Murray.
Ist. Lieut W. Quirke. U.S.A.
2nd, C. Meaney. Greenmount. Cork.

1921.

Capt. W Quirke. U.S.A.
Ist, Lieut. C Meaney.
2nd. " Frank Nolan. U.S.A.

1921.

Batt. O/C. Ed. Murray
Batt Adjt. John Ronhan.

1917/20.

Douglas Sluagh.
Capt. Sean Downey National
Army.
Liam. Foley. Passage. Co Cork.
1921.
M. Foley. Or B. Lyons.

Glasheen Sluagh.

1917/21.

O/C. P. Young. Now in National Army.
Vincent Morgan. Do.

~ 86 ~

Appendix 5 (Page 1)

SWORN STATEMENT MADE BEFORE ADVISORY COMMITTEE BY
CHRISTOPHER WOODS on 30th MAY 1939 - P.N. 27199.

Q. What is the name, please?
A. Christopher Woods.

Q. You joined the Fianna in Cork?
A. Yes.

Q. When?
A. About the end of 1916.

Q. When did you go to the Volunteers?
A. Between 1919 and 1920, I think.

Q. Up to your transfer to the Volunteers what was your job in
   the Fianna - usual Fianna training, was it?
A. Well, the usual Fianna training and my first job was the smash-
   ing of the recruiting office in Patrick St., and generally
   making a nuisance of ourselves; stopping soldiers and so forth
   and the W.A.A.C. - creating trouble, in other words.

Q. Did you have any rank in the Fianna?
A. At the time for a couple of months. I had previous training
   in the Hibernian Boys Brigade, and after a few months, I was
   section commander and after another few months I was Lt. which
   rank I held to the end of my Fianna service.

Q. Did you get any rank in the Volunteers before the Truce?
A. Yes. For about three months, I think, prior to the Truce, I
   was Coy. I.O. for "B" Coy., 1st Battalion, transferred from
   John Joe McCarthy, who was previous Coy. I.O., subject to full
   time Battalion I.O., Herbie Mahony.

5th Period.

When you went to "B" Coy. you say you were on general intelligence
   work?
A. Not exactly from the start but after a short time. That is
   the reason I was transferred, I think.

Q. What was the nature of the general intelligence work?
A. It covered everything. Suspects we got the names of to follow.

Q. In this year when you were transferred first?
A. Yes, I took my orders from my Coy. I.O. to shadow certain places
   or persons; keeping track of patrols - military or police. One
   particular man I spent a lot of time on was Ketchen, manager of
   Hipps.

Q. That was later?
A. Yes, I think when I was Company I.O. I would not be sure.

6th Period.

Q. Doing general intelligence work in "B" Coy. area?
A. Yes.

Q. And responsible for same to "B" Coy. I.O.?
A. Yes. That is John Joseph McCarthy.

Appendix 5 (Page 2)

2.

Q.. Up to the Truce on that Intelligence Officer work - what was it you were doing? Was it trailing suspects all the time?

A. Yes, and I took orders from my Coy. I.O. whatever job I was to do - trail a certain man, watch a certain Eks. or various other jobs.

Q. Did you have many suspects to watch?

A. We got different names of different people; people that were suspected of watching our fellows.

Q. Were you at work at the time?

A. Yes.

Q. What were you working at?

A. I was in Andy Daly's in Washington St.

Q. Shop assistant?

A. Yes, grocer's assistant.

Q. I suppose you have no references to hand in?

A. No, but I could have them if I wanted them.

Q. This work then was done after shop hours?

A. Yes, and say 4 or 5 nights a week and often during hours I often got reports into the shop. I was open at all times to take notes from this Herbert Mahoney.

7th Period.

Q. In the last few months you say you were responsible for working five Intelligence Officers from 1st May?

A. Yes. That was on the transfer of Mr. John Joe McCarthy. I don't know why but it was transferred to me from him. There may be a slight discrepancy in the dates there, because I was speaking to J.J. McCarthy and he makes out it was slightly later. He says about 17th May. Of course, I would not argue that point with him.

Q.. These fellows were assisting you?

A. These five I.O's of the names I gave there, yes.

Q. Did they bring reports to you in the shop or did you have to go around to them?

A. They brought reports to me - to my address mostly.

Q. And you co-ordinated them and sent them on?

A. Yes, and sent them on to McAuliffe; at least, addressed to McAuliffe, C/o Cawley in Washington St.

Q. Who was McAuliffe?

A. An assumed name for Mahoney.

Q. That was the Battalion I.O.?

A. Yes, that was the full time Battalion I.O.

Q. I see you took part in raids on postmen and taking of mails?

A. Yes. I had to be called out for that because they could not get the required number of men.

Q. How often did you do that?

A. That was the only one I remember.

Appendix 5 (Page 3)

3.

Q. Was it on the postman?
A. I actually took the mails from him. I was covered by armed men.

Q. You blocked roads for Blarney Barrack attack?
A. Yes, shifted carts and barrels and things from a farm on the top of Cloheen Road.

Q. Did you ever get any information that was of any value?
A. I cannot say I did, because all these things were taken out of my hands when I handed over these reports.

Q. Did you ever get any special information - any direct information yourself?
A. No.

Q. You were not in the way of having personal touch with any enemy agents or friends of agents?
A. No.

Q. Is there anything else about your service which you would like to add to that statement?
A. No, I think that about covers it in abstract.

Q. You never actually participated in any fight yourself before the Truce?
A. No.

Q. You didn't have to keep arms?
A. Yes, on a few occasions. I have a supplementary list.(handed in).

Q. What did you have to do with the burning of King St. Bks.?
A. I cannot say definitely but I was on the job on Union Hill. I think my purpose there was to inform the men employed on the actual burning of the arrival of the enemy.

Q. Were you armed?
A. No.

Q. Housed an armed party of 12 men on the occasion of the shooting of Sergt. Garvey?
A. Yes, the housing of the armed party is certain.

Q. How long had you got them?
A. All night.

Q. One night?
A. Yes.

Q. You were in the McSwiney bodyguard?
A. Yes, it was a funny thing for an I.O. but there was the Battn. I.O. Culhane there on the same night.

Q. You say W.J. Barry stayed in your home for 3 months?
A. Yes, I tried to get him this morning. He is teaching in the Westland Row school. I am sure he can verify that.

Q. Were the Tans looking for him?
A. Evidently.

Appendix 5 (Page 4)

Q. Cleaned rifles in Coy. dump?
A. Yes, one occasion.

Q. You say your home was open house for those doing their duty?
A. Yes.

Q. Held Intelligence meetings there?
A. Yes.

Q. And you had the Fianna Eireann training books and daggers?
A. Yes, that was during the Fianna period.

Q. You housed arms belonging to Bill Coyne?
A. Yes. I would refer that to "B" Coy. for actual verification because I don't know where the man is at the moment. He is believed to be in Dublin.

Q. You also stored "loot" which was got back after the burning of Cork?
A. Yes.

Q. Your home was raided?
A. Yes, on one occasion by the British military.

Q. You were not on the run yourself?
A. No.

8th Period.

Q. During the Truce what was the nature of the work? There was no camp service?
A. There was no active service at that time, except there was a little police work at that time.

Q. Did you go into any Bks.?
A. Yes. I had occasion to visit Tuckey St. Barracks and various Bks. around; all the other I.O's with me.

Q. You visited for I.O. purposes?
A. Yes, I did, yes, for information purposes. My father was Registrar of the Central Republican court which I helped him in. He is dead now.

9th Period.

Q. In the 9th period you claim that you were on Intelligence at Empress Place Bks., Cork?
A. Yes.

Q. You say that your service in Empress Place was full time, armed?
A. Yes.

Q. When?
A. The Coy. O./c. say the 1st. I think it is the 5th or 6th.

Q. Of July?
A. In May or June.

Q. You were there before the Truce ended then - before the Civil War started?
A. I could not answer that question, although I think I could say Yes, because I have a note here of when the Four Courts was shelled.

Appendix 5 (Page 5)

5.

Q. 28th June was the attack on the Four Courts?
A. I think I was in it previous to that.

Q. What was the duty there?
A. Full time. Men boarding the bouts to join up as Free State officers. One was a man named White. As far as I know he was an ex-British officer from Bantry. He had photographs and things of the different barracks in Cork. I captured him with another man by the name of Owen McCarthy.

Q. Did you get many of these fellows?
A. I got another man I was watching for a couple of days. I didn't actually get him - a man by the name of Courtney.

Q. You got one man?
A. I got another man as well, O'Connell -a fine Irish speaking man. I think he was a Limerick man. I had to fire on him to get him off the boat. I put him in Empress Place and some of the fellows were making a pass at him and I had to have him removed to Victoria Bks. where I thought he would be safer.

Q. While you were in this Bks. had you five fellows working under you?
A. No, only one man. His name was T. Moynihan.

Q. Were any of these men you held up - were they in the I.R.A. before the Truce?
A. I could not say that. I have an idea O'Connell was.

Q. Did you stay in Empress Place until evacuated?
A. Yes. The morning of the evacuation I got orders to go to Bishopstown and got a description of a suspect and was to bring him back dead or alive to Union Quay. There were a big lot of British soldiers whom I had shadowed for days previous in the South Mall, Cork, staying there. Picked up a lot of these fellows and got a lorry and they were shifted from there into Cork and from Cork into Blarney. Myself, I could not find this suspect I was after. He was supposed to be in a publichouse in Barretts in Bishopstown. When we got into town the Free State troops must have come into Douglas. I had three men with me. I got to Empress Place Bks. to find it was blown up. Went from that to Victoria Bks. and saw the O/c of the Bks. Went to Donoughmore to the dump. Stayed there for 2 or 3 days and we were about to be disarmed. I held my two guns and dumped them with two friends guns. I could give you that address.

Q. You did not have any actual encounter with Free State forces?
A. No.

Q. How long were you back in Cork before you were arrested?
A. I'd say about a week.

Q. Arrested on the 2nd September?
A. About the end of August, I'd say. I was a week at work, in any case, whether I was idle for a week previous to that or not I don't know.

Q. This was after coming back from Donoughmore?
A. Yes.

Q. Was it at your work you were arrested?
A. No.

Appendix 5 (Page 6)

6.

Q. You were not armed?
A. No. It was one Sunday evening.

Q. Where were you arrested?
A. At home, along with my two brothers.

Q. Were they taken too?
A. Yes.

Q. Were you interned then?
A. We were interrogatted by Sean Hales and Murphy from Bandon; threatened with mines and everything else.

Q. When did you get out - 20th April?
A. Yes.

Q. Did you sign a form?
A. Yes. It did not take anything from my principles.

Q. There was nothing doing when you came out, I suppose?
A. No.

MJG/AC

Appendix 5 (Page 7)

~~JANUARY~~, ~~1920~~ May 29th 1939

Supplementary List of Active Service

~~10 CUSTOMS?~~

Period 6 – Burning of King St. Barracks. Cork.
        Verified By Sean Lacey. 13. Company, 1st Batt, 1st Cork Brigade
        Old I·R·A men assc, Cork

Period 6 – Housed Armed Party of about 12 men on the occasion of
the shooting of Serg Garvey, Etc,
        Verified By Sean Lacey. Mossy Fitzgerald. as above address

Period 6 – I was one of the Bodyguard over the Remains of, Lord
Mayor McSweeny at Cork City Hall
        Verified By, Sean Lacey. as above address

On Intelligence I had help of Fianna Boys Murray, Kenneally

~~20 FRIDAY~~
        Their also (for 3 months) on the Run stayed at my home W.J. Barry
N.T. Foreman? of the Jury on inquest of Lord Mayor McCurtain

Period 6 – Cleaning Rifls at Company Dump "Delanys" Dublin Hill
        attended with company at funeral Lord Mayor McCurtain
        attended as Bodyguard at funeral Lord Mayor McSweeny

My Home (in heart of Enemy territory) was an open house for those
doing their duty in the I.R.A Cause, I at times held Intelligence
meetings there. also had there planted Fianna Eireann Training
Books, Daggers, Knuckledusters Seditious Literature Etc.
Also housed arms belonging Bill Coyne. B, Company 1st Batt
1st Cork Brigade, shifting in same from Augnes O'Connell Publican
Parnell Place, afterwards transferring same to a Barman in
~~P———~~ Public House in ~~———~~ Parliament St. Cork.
I also stored "loot" which I with others Retrieved from
"Looters" after the Burning of Cork. We were also
Raided, interrogated, searched, etc By British military.
My Father (R·I·P) was Registrar of Centre area. Cork
Republican Court. My Mother and Sister helped also in
arms Removing, mails Removing, All my Brothers[3] were active
members of Fianna Eireann and I,R,A.
My Service at Empress Place. Cork, was Full Time Armed

        Signed
        Christopher Woods
   Company I.O. B. Company. 1st Batt, 1st Cork Brigade

Appendix 6 (Page 1)

Fianna Éireann -- 1st Cork Brigade.

Brigade Staff.

Rank.	Name.	Present Address.
Comdt.	Frank McMahon.	Deceased.
Adjt.	Daniel Scully.	Derrynane, Turners Cross, Cork.
I.O.	Michael O'Leary,	England.(address not known)
Q.M.	Patrick Lynch	105 Commons Road, Cork.(see 'D' Coy.
		1st. Battalion)
Organiser	Jack Carey.	South Africa.(address not known)
O/C Cork City	Edward Gamble.	45 Grattan Street, Cork.

(Mr. Gamble claims to have been O/C Cork No.I. Brigade. We could get no confirm
Confirmation of this. We will not accept him as a verifying officer).
Your list also shows him as O/C 1st Battalion.

O/C A.S.U.	Stephen Walsh.	2 Hacketts Terrace, Lower Road, Cork.

Its 1st Battalion Staff.

Comdt.	Daniel Mulroy.	Deceased.
Adjt	Leo Cahill.	Loughlin, Carrigeen Park, Ballinlough Road, Cork.

(see 'E' No.I. 1st Battalion. L.Cahill was not appointed to the
Battalion Staff until the Truce period)

I.O.	Cornelius Curtin.	Deceased. (see 'G' Coy. 1st Battalion. He was

not appointed to the Battalion Staff until the Truce period).

Q.M.	See Q.M. Brigade Staff. and 'D(Coy. 1st Battalion.	

'A' Coy. 1st Battalion.

Capt.	Stephen Walsh,	2 Hacketts Terrace, Lower Road, Cork.
	(see O/C A.S.U. Brigade Staff).	
1st Lt.	J. Kelleher,	present address not known.
2nd. Lt.	Vincent O'Leary.	Dillions Cross, Cork.
Adjt.	James Fyne.	Deceased.
Q.M.	R. Busteed.	Deceased.
I.O.	P. Slattery.	
I.O.	P. Slattery.	Deceased.
I.O.	J. Phibbs,	? Oliver Plunket Street, Cork.

'B' Coy. 1st Battalion.

Capt.	Denis Woods,	c/o New Ireland Assurance Company,
		The Rock, Midleton, Co. Cork.
1st Lt.	Robert Flynn,	U.S.A.(address not known).
Adjt.	James Wickham,	Merchant's Quay, Cork.
Q.M.	John Caulfield.	63 Mount Eden Road, Cork.
I.O.	Thomas Carroll,	c/o C. O'Brien, Cycle Agent, Oliver Plunket St.
I.O.	Cornelius Kenneally,	England.

'C' Coy. 1st Battalion.

Capt.	John Murray,	124. Blarney Street, Cork.
Capt.	Cornelius O'Leary,	England.
Lt.		
Adjt.		
Q.M.		
I.O.		
I.O.		

'E' Coy. 1st Battalion.

Capt.	Stephen Wall,	Deceased.
Capt.	Patrick Lynch,	(see Brigade and 1st Battalion Q.M.)
	Mr. Lynch was O/C 'D' Coy. up to the Truce.	
Lt.	P.J. Cronin...	present address not known.
Adjt.	F.McCarthy,	present address not known.
I.O.	V. Foley,	present address not known.
I.O.	T. Barrett,	2 Hawthorn Villas, South Douglas Road, Cork.

We are not prepared to accept that Mr. Barrett was a member of the Fianna
prior to the Truce.

Appendix 6 (Page 2)

Fianna Eireann---   2.   Cork No.I. Brigade. Contd.

'E' No.N Coy. 1st Battalion.

Capt.   Leo Cahill, Loughlin, Carrigeen Park, Ballinlough Road, Cork
           (see Adjt. 1st Battalion,).
1st Lt.   Vincent Stack, England, present address not known.
           V. Stack was not appointed Coy. O/C until after the Truce.
Lt. & Q.M. M. O'Neill,   address not known.
Adjt.   T. Burns,   could get no information regarding this man.

'E' No.2. Coy. 1st Battalion.

Capt.   Tadgh Forde, Deceased. was O/C in 1920.
Capt.   John Feley, 56 Dublin Street, Cork. O/C in 1921.
1st. Lt.   John McCarthy,   Deceased.
2nd. Lt.   Denis O'Mahony, 34 Guildford Road, Seven Kings, Illford, England.
Q.M.   James OLeary, Upper Dublin Hill, Cork.
I.O.   Jerimiah Murphy, Upper John Street, Cork.
Your list shows the officers as in 1920.

'G' Coy. 1st Battalion.

Capt.   Daniel Gamble, c/o Mr.D.Long, Orrery Road, Cork.
Lt.&Capt. Jerimiah Pierce,   Deceased.
Adjt.   Leo Cahill, Clay, U.S.A.
Q.M.   Cornelius Curtin, Deceased, (was appointed Battalion I.O. during
                        the Truce.
I.O.   Robert Boyle,   Dagenham, Essex, England.
I.O.   George Hurley,   38a McCurtain's Buildings, College Road, Cork.

'H' Coy. 1st Battalion.

Capt.   Peter Young,   Deceased.
Capt.   D.V.(Vincent) Horgan,Comdt. Army Air Corps, Gormanstown Air Station.
1st Lt.   Edward Uniacke,2 St. Josephs View, College Road, Cork.
2nd Lt.   James Cross,   Deceased.
Q.M.   Michael Callinan, Deceased.
Adjt.   Edward Warren,   7 Leitrim Street, Cork.

Note. We suggest that Messrs. Leo Cahill, John Foley, John Murray and
D.V. Horgan,Comdt. be accepted as verifying officers for the 1st Battalion.

'C' Company, 1st Battalion, will be completed at a later date.

Fianna Eireann--------Cork No. I. Brigade.

2nd Battalion Staff.

Comdt.	Edward Murray,	School Place, Cathedral Road, Cork.
Adjt.	J. Roynane,	Deceased.
Q.M.	T. Donovan,	
I.O.	William Quirke,	31 Stewart Street, Brooklyn, New York, U.S.A.

This appointment was not filled until the Truce period.
see 'C' Coy. 2nd. Battalion.

'B' Coy. 2nd Battalion.

Capt.	Richard O'Leary,	Ringmahon, Blackrock, Cork.
Lt.	James Delea,	Blackrock, Cork.
Adjt.	W ? Donovan,	
I.O.	M. Kenny,	Back Road, Riverstown, Glanmire, Co. Cork.

'C' Coy. 2nd Battalion.

Capt.	William Quirke,	U.S.A. see Battalion Staff.
Lt.&Adjt.	J. Donovan,	England.
I.O.	J. McCarthy,	present address not known.
Q.M.	George Mc Hugh,	England.

'D' Coy. 2nd Battalion.

Capt.	Sean Downey,	Deceased.

(all other officers of this Company were not appointed until after the Truce.)

Lt & Adjt.	D. Fitzgibbon.	Ballincurrig Park, Douglas, Cork.
I.O. & Q.M.	J. Morley,	Deceased.

'E' Coy. 2nd Battalion.

Capt.	Frank Nolan,	U.S.A.
Lt.	~~~~~~~~~~~~~~~~~~~~~~~~~~~~~~~~~~~~~~~	
Adjt.	T. Donovan	
Q.M.	Richard Power.	
I.O.	P Manning,	Deceased.

'F' Coy. 2nd Battalion.

Capt.	Christopher Hurley,	55 Kent Road, Ballyphehane, Cork.
Lt.	William Rose,	present address not known.
2nd Lt.	William Downey,	63 Thomas Davis Street, Cork.
Adjt	Timothy Donovan,	117 Evergreen Road, Cork.
Q.M.	J. Fennell,	Dublin, address not known.

Your list shows T. Donovan as Coy. Captain, this is not correct.(see Adjt.)
" "   "   R.O'Mahony as Adjt, this appointment was made during the Truce.

I.O.	see Lieutenants appointment.Wm. Rose	
I.O.	J. Griffin,	no information available , doubtful if such a person was a member of this Company.

Capt.	Richard Noonan	Deceased.

Lt.&Q.M. No information as to who held this appointment, doubtful if it was filled.

Lt.& I.O. as for Lt. & Q.M.
Adjt, as above.

'H' Coy. 2nd Battalion.

Capt.	Charles Meaney,	2 Ettie Ville, Magazine Road, Cork.
Lt.	J. Cuttin,	7 Greenmount Avenue, Cork.
Adjt.	J. Roynane, Deceased,	see Battalion Adjt.
Q.M.	this appointment was not filled.	

I.O.(see Company Captain, your list shows C. Meaney as I.O. Its the same person.)

Note. We would suggest that Mr E. Murray and Mr. C. Meaney be accepted as verifying officers for the 2nd Battalion.

Printed in Great Britain
by Amazon